Heidegger's Life and Thought

Heidegger's Life and Thought

A Tarnished Legacy

Mahon O'Brien

**ROWMAN &
LITTLEFIELD**
INTERNATIONAL
London • New York

Published by Rowman & Littlefield International Ltd
6 Tinworth Street, London SE11 5AL
www.rowmaninternational.com

Rowman & Littlefield International Ltd is an affiliate of
Rowman & Littlefield
4501 Forbes Boulevard, Suite 200, Lanham, Maryland 20706, USA
With additional offices in Boulder, New York, Toronto (Canada), and London (UK)
www.rowman.com

Copyright © Mahon O'Brien, 2020

All rights reserved. No part of this book may be reproduced in any form or by any electronic or mechanical means, including information storage and retrieval systems, without written permission from the publisher, except by a reviewer who may quote passages in a review.

British Library Cataloguing in Publication Information
A catalogue record for this book is available from the British Library

ISBN: HB 978-1-78661-382-0
ISBN: PB 978-1-78661-383-7

Library of Congress Cataloging-in-Publication Data Available

ISBN: 978-1-78661-382-0 (cloth)
ISBN: 978-1-78661-383-7 (pbk.)
ISBN: 978-1-78661-384-4 (electronic)

For Jim and Una

Contents

Acknowledgements		vii
Preface		ix
1	Ways Not Works	1
2	Early Life	7
3	Rumours of the Hidden King	19
4	The Hidden King Returns to Freiburg	27
5	The 1930s: Politics, Art and Poetry	55
6	The Nazi Rector	71
7	Return from Syracuse	79
8	Heidegger 'Abroad'	99
9	The Final Years	107
10	Heidegger's Legacy	111
Sources		119
Index		123

Acknowledgements

I am very fortunate to work in a vibrant and collegial academic environment in the School of History, Art History and Philosophy at the University of Sussex. I am grateful to everyone in the Philosophy Department in particular who have been wonderful colleagues. I am especially grateful to Anthony Booth and Gordon Finlayson who have been the best of colleagues and friends since I came to the University of Sussex and to Christos Hadjioannou who completed his doctoral studies here a couple of years ago. I would also like to thank the many gifted graduate and undergraduate students who worked on Heidegger's notoriously difficult texts with me in seminars and lectures in Existentialism, Phenomenology, Continental Aesthetics, Figures in Post-Kantian Philosophy and Modern European Philosophy. Tom Bunyard was kind enough to read an earlier draft of the manuscript with some of his colleagues and graduate students at Brighton University. Their feedback and comments were extremely helpful. I am also grateful to the anonymous reviewers who offered a lot of constructive and insightful feedback. I would also like to thank Frankie Mace, commissioning editor at Rowman & Littlefield International, for believing in this little book from the beginning.

I remain indebted to my family, in particular my mother and father, Jim and Una, who gave me the opportunity to pursue the life I have wanted to lead from the very beginning and who continue to make the family homes in Ireland and Lanzarote places of love and laughter for me, my brother, my sister and nieces. I would also like to thank Ana, who brings light and joy to every moment of every day, and Daisy, who inspires both of us with her constant curiosity. In closing I should like to give thanks once more for the peace and tranquillity that our family home in the valley offers; this is the third time I have written acknowledgements for a book in the house where I grew up, and I remain more grateful for this gift of my placed history than ever!

Preface

No other figure in the history of philosophy has proved as controversial or managed to divide opinion so much as a man from the Black Forest in Germany who died in 1976. His name was Martin Heidegger and, depending on who you are talking to, he is either the greatest scourge to have ever afflicted academic philosophy or, conversely, the most important philosopher to have emerged from the Western tradition since Hegel. This situation is not exactly ameliorated by the fact that Heidegger was a committed and outspoken member of the Nazi party in the early 1930s in particular and indeed became the Nazi rector of Freiburg University in 1933, a mere four years after he had assumed the chair previously occupied by his one-time mentor and friend, the famous phenomenologist, Edmund Husserl, who was himself a Jew. Not alone that, and contrary to the official story peddled by Heidegger himself from the time of the denazification proceedings brought against him after the end of the Second World War, Heidegger's association with National Socialism was neither brief nor incidental to his thought. Indeed he insisted to some of his closest friends and colleagues that his commitment to National Socialism was based on some of the core elements of his magnum opus—*Being and Time*.

Over the last five years or so the Heidegger controversy has flared up with a vengeance as Heidegger's philosophical notebooks[1] from the 1930s and 1940s have begun to appear; and, within these notebooks (along with some important seminars and lecture courses from the 1930s, which have also been published recently) it is patently obvious that Heidegger's unsavoury political outlook (which should not be straightforwardly conflated with historical National Socialism) is something he is looking to map onto his philosophy in some way, shape or form.

Notwithstanding, and despite the noisy protestations of opportunistic opponents of Heidegger's philosophy and influence, it would be precipitous in the extreme to recommend the extirpation of Heidegger's thought from the canon.[2] Heidegger is, without question, one of the most important philosophers of the twentieth century, and his thought has had a profound impact on the trajectory of philosophy during the second half of that century and continues to prove hugely influential for philosophers today. Contemporary continental philosophy is indelibly marked by Heidegger's influence, which has had far-reaching implications for phenomenology, hermeneutics, existentialism, deconstruction, aesthetics, the history of philosophy and philosophy of technology along with having been hugely influential for literature, the arts, theology, architecture and psychoanalytic theory. The idea then that one should simply strike Heidegger's name from the canon and ignore his work betrays a profound ignorance of the magnitude of Heidegger's intellectual achievements, not least since it presumes that many of the most important intellectual figures from the second half of the twentieth century right through to today, who acknowledge a major intellectual debt to Heidegger, were either too blind or too stupid to notice that Heidegger's philosophy is simply the abstruse mysticism of a charlatan or the work of a dangerous Nazi hack looking, as one commentator argues,[3] to surreptitiously inscribe Nazism into the history of Western philosophy.

In this short introductory text, I have tried to offer a simple, jargon-free introduction to Heidegger's life and thought—warts and all. Some Heidegger scholars want to veto all discussion of Heidegger's politics and insist on a sharp division between his philosophy and his political views; however, even if this were not in part a biographical work, Heidegger's political views and his philosophy would still need to be considered side by side since I don't agree that the separation of the two can be executed quite so neatly as these commentators suggest. It is Heidegger himself who wedded his thought to his own interpretation of Nazi ideology—and we might as well accept that fact and then consider whether, ultimately, it undermines his philosophy or simply calls parts of it into question.[4]

Again, it is important to emphasise that this is an *introductory* work and, as such, does not pretend to offer sophisticated, technical or exhaustive treatments of Heidegger's texts. My aim in this book is to introduce readers to a famous twentieth-century philosopher whom they may already have heard of and would like to learn a little more about. Thus, it is best to consider this book an accessible and general introduction to the life and thought of Martin Heidegger. I have also tried to offer an honest and frank portrait of the man and his work. It is important that people coming to Heidegger for the first time are not presented with an overly sanitised account of this complex character. Heidegger managed to inspire almost cult-like devotion during his own lifetime and can sometimes have a similar effect on scholars who have been influenced by his work in more recent times. Some of these commentators have been guilty of all kinds of intellectual acrobatics and apologetics in an attempt to rehabilitate Heidegger's image both for philosophers and the wider intellectual community. However, it seems to me that one does Heidegger studies a disservice in camouflaging his many deplorable faults in both his professional and his personal life. Rather, what is needed is an honest portrait of this fascinating but deeply flawed human being while underlining his continuing importance as a philosopher today. Heidegger was neither a hero nor a saint, and he should not be presented as such since those kinds of misrepresentations will only serve to confuse and potentially alienate prospective readers of Heidegger who will eventually learn for themselves that Heidegger was a Nazi and a selfish, arrogant egomaniac to boot.

Heidegger's body of work is vast, and it would be next to impossible to do justice to the breadth of his philosophical interests and contributions. However, pretty much everything he wrote about and discussed was in some way related to his lifelong concern with the question of the meaning of being. My own view is that Heidegger's first efforts to inquire into the question concerning the meaning of being anticipate most of the decisive moves he makes over the decades following the publication of his most important and influential book, *Being and Time*. Consequently, readers will find here an interpretation of Heidegger that presents his work as a continuous, evolving, if not entirely seamless, enterprise. This is not an uncontroversial way to read Heidegger; but it is the interpretation of his thinking which he continually seems to favour and the one which, in my view at least, has the least number of inconsistencies and infelicities to explain away to the discerning reader. This is an introduction, then, to Heidegger's progressive paths of thought spanning roughly sixty years.

NOTES

1. The *Black Notebooks* (*Schwarze Hefte*) are so named as a result of the black oilcloth covers as opposed to the sinister nature of some of the content.
2. This is essentially the recommendation of Emmanuel Faye in his book on the Heidegger controversy (see Faye, 2009).
3. This is one of the central claims that Emmanuel Faye tries to defend.

4. In a controversial and provocative book, which followed hot on the heels of the publication of the first three volumes of Heidegger's *Black Notebooks*, Peter Trawny takes on some of these questions in the context of the most problematic passages from the notebooks. His findings are often alarming but certainly merit attention and cannot be dismissed or ignored (see Trawny, 2015).

ONE
Ways Not Works

The question as to how Heidegger should be 'classified' or whether we can associate him with a particular school or movement in philosophy is, itself, something of a hornet's nest of difficulties. Heidegger is notoriously difficult to 'label' or categorise; he eschews all labels and schools, even though he explicitly wears the influences of other philosophers and styles of thinking on his sleeve. For example, even if Heidegger owes a certain intellectual debt to Husserl and looks to inaugurate his own brand of phenomenology for a period of time, it would be misleading to class Heidegger as a phenomenologist in an unqualified way.[1] Of course, in many ways, Heidegger remains close to phenomenology in terms of 'method' (although even 'method' is too robust a description), but it is a mistake to simply see Heidegger's work as a contribution to Husserlian phenomenology or indeed, to dismiss works like *Being and Time*, for example, as simply Husserl 'gone wrong', or, as Husserl himself rather flat-footedly suggested, an elaboration of life in the natural attitude. And, of course, there are also those who insist that anything of merit in Heidegger's apparently novel attempt at a phenomenology in *Being and Time* is simply a recapitulation or reprisal of ideas to be found in Husserl's earlier work. This itself is part of a pattern of criticism that has continually emerged in response to Heidegger's work. Generations of critics of *Being and Time* in particular have sought to dismiss Heidegger's work as hopelessly derivative—a mere collage or patchwork of themes and ideas lifted from Aristotle, Kant, Husserl, Kierkegaard, Luther, Dilthey—what have you. The preponderance of these criticisms are, I would submit, excessively reductive; Heidegger very obviously employs and exploits themes, images and ideas from his own unique philosophical heritage—there are unmistakable Aristotelian, Kantian, Kierkegaardian and Husserlian elements in *Being and Time*; there are traces of lesser known philosophical figures that would have exercised an influence on the younger Heidegger as well; but it is deeply misleading to suggest that Heidegger's extraordinary book, published in 1927, amounts to nothing more than a reproduction of some or all of the ideas of any or all of his influences.

We will discuss Heidegger's 1927 masterpiece shortly; however, in relation to how one 'classifies' Heidegger's work, an important problem already emerges in terms of how one should understand *Being and Time* in the broader context of Heidegger's work as a whole. Many critics are keen to divide Heidegger's work into distinct periods with his early work—which, they insist, he subsequently eschews—dominated in particular by the anthropologically oriented existential phenomenology of *Being and Time*. His thinking then changes and evolves into the 'later Heidegger', or what is sometimes characterised as 'Heidegger II'.[2] Heidegger himself insists that one should look on his progressive, lifelong efforts as 'ways' not 'works'. And yet, even some of those Heideggerians who profess to do as much nevertheless insist on an overly rigid and, in my view, misguided and disjointed way of interpreting Heidegger's relentless efforts to return to the *Seinsfrage* (question of being or being-question). Heidegger poses this question at the beginning of *Being and Time* and he insists that it is the question that 'was' and 'remained' his question for the rest of his career—namely, the question concerning the meaning of being. As Heidegger himself insists in one of many such retrospectives on his work,

> The question concerning the "meaning" [of being], i.e., in accordance with the elucidation in *Being and Time*, the question concerning grounding the domain of projecting-open—and then, the question of the truth of be-ing—is and remains my question, and is my one and only question; for this question concerns what is most sole and unique. In the age of total lack of questioning anything, it is sufficient as a start to inquire into the question of all questions. (CP, 8)

Heidegger then, in *Being and Time*, and *for the rest of his career* is interested in the way being becomes meaningful and attempts to find an appropriate way to ask the associated questions. He describes this as an attempt to find a 'way' and insists that his 'corpus' is more aptly characterised as a series of 'ways' not 'works'. Indeed, one of Heidegger's most famous collections of essays is called *Pathmarks* (*Wegmarken*)—the idea being that his thinking proceeds along various pathways. Heidegger had obviously come to believe that his first attempt to find a 'way' in *Being and Time* was limited in certain respects, and he never 'officially' returns to finish the project which he had first set out as a blueprint for something much larger than the actual published version of *Being and Time*. However, the 'shortcomings' of *Being and Time* have often been overstated. Rather than seeing how Heidegger is already paving the way for and setting in motion a chain of lifelong paths of inquiry, some critics and commentators have foisted a whole range of artificial interpretations on that work which obscure the manner in which *Being and Time* and the attempt at a fundamental ontology represent the beginning of a lifelong pursuit of the being-question.

In a number of his posthumously published writings, we frequently find Heidegger fulminating against misreadings of *Being and Time*. And, indeed, even today one is wont to find established Heidegger scholars railing against the dead-born nature of Heidegger's early project as a 'Dasein-oriented' story.[3] By this, they mean that Heidegger's early work is a kind of humanist, anthropological or excessively subjectivist attempt to inquire after the question concerning the meaning of being, one which distorts the results of the inquiry and leads Heidegger to abandon his early attempts and take up the posture and rhetoric that is then associated with Heidegger II. Heidegger repeatedly rails against such interpretations of *Being and Time* which, again, overlook the context of Heidegger's inquiries into our everyday existence and the historical, temporal backdrop to that existence. Heidegger is not interested in commenting on the human condition in particular, though, of course, he is not oblivious to the fact that his inquiries have profound consequences for how we understand the nature of our own existence. Rather, he is interested in examining this existence for clues concerning the manner in which being becomes meaningful for human beings with a view to getting some traction on what the meaning of being itself might be. In his recently published notebooks from the 1930s, for example, we find Heidegger speaking of the necessity of countering the misreadings of *Being and Time* in this manner and the 'perverted labelling of my endeavors as "philosophy of existence" or "existential philosophy"' (*Ponderings II–VI*, 25). He goes on to bemoan the destitution of the interpretations of *Being and Time* (a recurring complaint one finds in Heidegger's reflections and self-interpretations following the publication of his 1927 masterpiece): 'People are waiting for the second volume of *Being and Time*; I am waiting for this waiting to cease and for people to finally confront the first volume' (*Ponderings II–VI*, 135). And again, later in his notebooks, we find Heidegger dismissing the book's conventional reception:

> *Being and Time* is not a 'philosophy of time' and even less a doctrine about the 'temporality' [*Zeitlichkeit*] of humans; on the contrary, it is clearly and surely *one* way toward the exposition of the ground of the truth of being—the truth of *being itself* and not of beings, not even of beings *as* beings. The guideline is a leap in advance into 'primordial temporality' [*Temporalitaet*], that in which originary time along with originary space essentially occur together *as* unfoldings of the essence of truth, unfoldings of the transporting-captivating clearing and concealment of truth.
>
> Admittedly the insufficient first draft of the Third Division of Part I on 'time and being,' had to be eradicated. A critically-historically configured reflection of it is contained in the lecture course of [summer semester] 1927. (*Ponderings II–VI*, 199–200)

This perpetual attempt to pursue the being-question results in a non-systematic and often highly experimental and unconventional series of 'pathways'. Heidegger is not trying to build a system or write treatises, and so his thinking remains defiantly non-systematic, resisting any kind of easy reduction to a 'school' of thinking. It is difficult then to establish or identify a 'doctrine' or 'theory' that we could label as 'Heideggerian'. As Heidegger himself insists in 1966, in a letter addressed to one of the early North American Heidegger symposia (which were the forerunners to what soon became the Heidegger Circle)—the *Seinsfrage*, that is, the question concerning the meaning of being, is what calls for thinking—not Heidegger himself:

> I would be very glad if it were possible to orient the discussion at once—in the first moments of the symposium—purely and decisively toward the subject matter itself. In that way there would develop, instead of a 'Heidegger Symposium,' a *Consultation on the Being-question* [*Seinsfrage*]. For it is this question—and it alone—that determines the way of my thought and its limits. (Richardson, 1993, 17)

In his commentary on the same letter, Richardson notes,

> What is interesting about this letter is not its substance but its emphasis. As a matter of fact, nothing that is said here is new. We

all know very well that from the very beginning of the way, Heidegger's question—the only one—has been the question about the meaning of Being. (21–22)

So, even though the distinction between Heidegger I and Heidegger II (which Richardson himself coined) has sometimes led to the belief that Heidegger II exists at the expense of Heidegger I, Richardson himself seems committed to a much more moderate view and underlines here the continuous nature of Heidegger's lifelong pursuit of the being-question.

NOTES

1. Edmund Husserl is credited with inaugurating that school of philosophy still referred to as phenomenology today. Husserl was certainly not the first philosopher to use the term and some of his most crucial insights can be traced to Franz Brentano whose lectures he attended. Phenomenology still ranks as one of the dominant schools in contemporary philosophy and Husserl's pioneering efforts continue to shape the ideas of thinkers working from within that school. Phenomenologists, as the name implies, are interested in studying phenomena. Phenomenon derives from the Ancient Greek word *phainomenon* which means 'appearance'. Kant had famously distinguished between the phenomenon and the noumenon in his *Critique of Pure Reason*, and this distinction is one which the phenomenologist is taking up in a way. That is, we should not confuse our claims about the things we experience, and thus the manner and ways in which things appear to us, as tantamount to making claims about the nature of things in themselves. In Husserl's case, he believes that what is needed is an exhaustive account of the structures and patterns of those same experiences which could, in turn, serve as a foundation for all scientific inquiry.
2. William Richardson's monumental study, *Heidegger: Through Phenomenology to Thought*, was one of the first and, for many, remains the definitive study of Heidegger's philosophy in the English language. It was Richardson who first coined the distinction between Heidegger I and Heidegger II. Despite the fact that Heidegger explicitly distances himself from the way scholars conceive of the split between 'Heidegger I' and 'Heidegger II', a number of Heideggerians have been trenchant in their support for a circumscription of Heidegger's work whereby Heidegger II involves the rejection of Heidegger I.
3. *Dasein* is a German word that Heidegger uses in a very particular way in *Being and Time* and which, for the most part, is not translated into English. Heidegger's use of the term is not typical, and while the term is understood to mean 'existence' in ordinary German, Heidegger wants to use the term *instead* of traditional terms like 'subject', 'human being' or 'person'. Heidegger emphasises the use of the term *sein* (to be) itself as part of the term *Dasein* and it is probably best understood in English as meaning 'being-here', although the *da* in *Dasein* could also be translated as 'there'. Having said as much, 'here' or 'there' are somewhat misleading as well insofar as they don't convey the dynamic, non-static nature of our thrown awareness.

TWO

Early Life

Martin Heidegger was born on 26 September 1889 in the small town of Messkirch in the Black Forest region of Germany. The details of a philosopher's birth might not seem particularly significant; however, in the case of Heidegger, we cannot overstate the importance of his birthplace and homeland to the development of his thought. Some might argue that there was an element of self-staging in this. As Theodor Adorno[1] colourfully points out in some of his polemics against Heidegger, there is no denying Heidegger's penchant for posturing as a self-styled philosopher peasant, a self-portrait he frequently pitted against the vacuous urbanity of cosmopolitan life and the inauthentic philosophising he associated with it. Heidegger's sense of belonging to his native region and its heritage, however, was also something that chimed with a commitment to some rather worrisome sentiments that permeated his confrontation with modernity in ways that many commentators have failed to diagnose. The irony of Heidegger's introduction to a lecture course on Aristotle might not be lost on the reader here in that Heidegger famously declared: 'Regarding the personality of a philosopher, our only interest is that he was born at a certain time, that he worked and that he died. The character of the philosopher, and issues of that sort, will not be addressed here' (Heidegger, 2009, 4). There is no doubt that Heidegger would have rightly encouraged his students to avoid becoming entangled with the concerns of biographers and to focus instead on what for him remained vital, namely,

Aristotle's thought. As he remarks somewhat bitterly in his notebooks:

> Would that a thoughtful grounding again became a sort of compilation of dicta, well protected against idle talk and unharmed by all hurried misinterpretation; would that opera omnia of twenty or more volumes along with the concomitant snooping into the author's life and the gathering of his casual utterances (I mean the usual 'biographies' and collections of correspondence) would disappear, and the work itself be strong enough and be kept free of the disfavour of being explained through a bringing in of the 'personal', i.e., kept from being dissolved into generalities. (*Ponderings II–VI*, 238–39)

Notwithstanding, Heidegger himself makes it very clear that the biographical details of his own life, in particular the Alemannian-Swabian region from which he came, his historical background and heritage, were all crucial to an understanding of the manner in which his thinking developed.[2] In his first major and, without question his most important and influential work, *Being and Time*, Heidegger distances himself from some of his intellectual predecessors, notably Kant and Husserl, precisely because of their failure to recognise the role of one's specificity and historical situation to philosophical inquiry. In some of his letters from as early as 1916, we see Heidegger criticise both Kant and Husserl in this regard for what he takes to be their anaemic formalism. In a letter to his then fiancé, Elfride, from March of that year Heidegger writes:

> today I know that there <u>can</u> be a philosophy of vibrant life [*des lebendigen Lebens*] — that I <u>can</u> declare war on rationalism right through to the bitter end — without falling victim to the anathema of unscientific thought — I <u>can</u> — I <u>must</u> — & so I'm today faced by the necessity of the problem: how is philosophy to be produced as living truth & as creation of the personality valuably and powerfully.
>
> The Kantian question is not only <u>wrongly</u> put — it fails to capture the problem; this is much richer and deeper.
>
> We must not give our heroes stones instead of bread when they come back hungry from the battlefield, not unreal and dead categories, not shadowy forms and bloodless compartments in which to keep a life ground down by rationalism neat and tidy and let it moulder away. (LW, 17)

The following year, Heidegger writes to Elfride in a similar vein but with his criticisms aimed this time at Husserl:

> I cannot accept Husserl's phen[omenology]. as a final position even if it joins up with philos.—because in its approach & accordingly in its goal it is too narrow & bloodless & because such an approach cannot be made absolute. Life is too rich & too great— thus—for relativities that seek to come close to its meaning (that of the absolute) in the form of philosophical systems, it's a question of discovering the liberating path in an absolute articulation of relativity. . . . The implacable necessity of a comparable engagement cannot be evaded today. . . . Since I've been lecturing, up to now I've constantly experienced these sudden reversals— until 'historical man' came to me in a flash this winter. (LW, 33)

In some ways, perhaps, Heidegger was an unlikely candidate for a career in academia. For one thing, he was born into a family of relatively modest means:

> The Heideggers were not affluent, but neither were they poor. Two thousand marks in immovable assets and a 960-mark income tax assessment (in 1903) put them in the lower middle class. This was enough for a family to live on, but not enough for the children to receive expensive higher education. At that point the Church lent a hand. It was the Church's usual practice to support gifted youngsters and at the same time recruit future priests, especially in rural regions. (Safranski, 1998, 9)

Heidegger's father was a cooper and sexton of the Catholic Church in Messkirch, and his mother, a good-natured and alacritous woman by all accounts, came from a farming background, and Heidegger would have spent a good deal of his childhood summers on the family farm. Heidegger retained strong ties with the countryside and the peasant farming communities he identified with; indeed, Heidegger developed a keen distrust of city life and the inherent cosmopolitanism and bourgeois decadence he associated it with. In a letter to Elfride dated 21 July 1918, when Heidegger was still on military duty, he recounts in horror the scene that greeted him and a comrade when they spent some of their free time visiting Berlin.

> Yesterday evening we did something special, travelled to Berlin & had a look at the bustle on Friedrichstrasse—we didn't have the courage to go into a bar—at half past 11 we came home again, both of us disgusted to the marrow—I presume we only saw the surface—but it is wilder than I could have imagined. I'd never have believed such an atmosphere of artificially cultivated, most vulgar and sophisticated sexuality was possible, but now I do understand Berlin better—the character of Friedrichstrasse has

rubbed off on the whole city—& in such a milieu there can be no true intellectual culture—a priori there cannot—& even if every perfect remedy were to hand—it lacks what is simply Great and Divine. When I think of Freibg. [Freiburg] & its Minster & the outlines of the Black Forest mountains—! The war hasn't yet become frightful enough for us. The people here have lost their soul—their faces don't have any expression at all—at most one of vulgarity, there's no staying this decadence now—perhaps the 'spirit' of Berlin can be overcome by a home-grown culture at the provincial universities—at any rate our youth will only be restored to health from this quarter—<u>if it's possible at all</u>. (LW, 45)

Heidegger remained inimical to urban life to the very end and took every possible opportunity to retreat to the hut in Todtnauberg[3] to work in peace and solitude, breaking occasionally to converse or socialise with the local farmers, chopping wood, smoking pipes and generally trying to immerse himself in the life of a Black Forest peasant farmer. Heidegger would go so far as to characterise his own philosophical labours as of a piece with the daily toil of the neighbouring peasants.

> And this philosophical work does not take its course like the aloof studies of some eccentric. It belongs right in the midst of the peasant's work. When the young farm boy drags his heavy sled up the slope and guides it, piled high with beech logs, down the dangerous descent to his house, when the herdsman, lost in thought and slow of step, drives his cattle up the slope, when the farmer in his shed gets the countless shingles ready for his roof, my work is of the same sort. It is intimately rooted in and related to the life of the peasants.
>
> A city-dweller thinks he has 'gone out among the people' as soon as he condescends to have a long conversation with a peasant. But in the evening during a work-break, when I sit with the peasants by the fire or at the table in the 'Lord's Corner', we mostly say nothing at all. We smoke our pipes in silence. Now and again someone might say that the woodcutting in the forest is finishing up, that a marten broke into the hen-house last night, that one of the cows will probably calf in the morning, that someone's uncle suffered a stroke, that the weather will soon turn. The inner relationship of my own work to the Black Forest and its people comes from a centuries-long and irreplaceable rootedness in the Alemannian-Swabian soil. (WP, 28)

Heidegger goes on to lament the philosophical and spiritual destitution of the city in contrast to the rural world which, he believed, nourished his thinking and remembers, as an example, an elderly peasant neighbour:

> In the public world one can be made a 'celebrity' overnight by the newspapers and journals. That always remains the surest way to have ones' ownmost intentions get misinterpreted and quickly and thoroughly forgotten.
>
> In contrast, the memory of the peasant has its simple and sure fidelity which never forgets. Recently an old peasant woman up there was approaching death. She liked to chat with me frequently, and she told me many old stories of the village. In her robust language, full of images, she still preserved many old words and various sayings which have become unintelligible to the village youth today and hence are lost to the spoken language. Very often in the past year when I lived alone in the cabin for weeks on end, this peasant woman with her 83 years would still come climbing up the slope to visit me. She wanted to look in from time to time, as she put it, to see whether I was still there or whether 'someone' had stolen me off unawares. She spent the night of her death in conversation with her family. Just an hour and a half before the end she sent her greetings to the 'Professor.' Such a memory is worth incomparably more than the most astute report by any international newspaper about my alleged philosophy. (WP, 28–29)

Indeed, as an emerging philosopher and lecturer, Heidegger was already known for his rather eccentric sartorial habits—sometimes arriving to his lectures in his skiing gear or dressed as a Swabian peasant. There is no doubt that this was all very much part of an image that Heidegger carefully crafted and cultivated. After all, he was not a farmer, he didn't come from a peasant family and he spent all of his adult life in academic and intellectual circles. Nevertheless, it would be unfair perhaps to ridicule his posturing excessively—Heidegger genuinely felt intellectually revitalised during his frequent sojourns in Todtnauberg. It became a place of refuge for Heidegger and, indeed, an intellectual retreat where he completed much of the work which propelled him to international fame. Having said as much, Heidegger's suspicion of cosmopolitanism and his glorification of all things agrarian bordered on the fanatical at times. Heinrich Petzet also remarks on this feature of Heidegger's personality.

> Heidegger was slightly suspicious of everything that had to do with the city and never quite felt comfortable in it, except in the only city that received his undivided sympathy. In simply get-

> ting close to a big city—with its proliferating dump sites, factories, and desolate housing developments, with the whole ugly atmosphere of formless and rampant growth that surrounds even old and beautiful cities—Heidegger, an extremely sensitive man, would be affected with almost physical abhorrence. . . . If Heidegger lacked a certain 'urbanity' and was estranged from everything pertaining to city life, this was particularly so in the case of the urbane spirit of the Jewish circles in the large cities of the West.[4] (Petzet, 1993, 33–34)

Like so many aspects of his life, however, Heidegger tried to justify his own private proclivities philosophically, which leads to all manner of interpretive difficulties since one has to constantly repel errant criticisms of his work. Such criticisms, focusing on the irrational ways he sometimes tried to use his philosophy to justify ridiculous views, look to throw the baby out with the bathwater, not recognising that some of the philosophical ideas to which Heidegger attaches his prejudices and preferences are, nevertheless, not without merit.

By the time Heidegger was at the peak of his philosophical powers, he had become a celebrity courted by intellectuals, artists, poets and philosophers from all over the world. It's not clear that Heidegger's fame ever sat comfortably with him. That is not to say that Heidegger was modest or humble; granted, he feigned humility at times, but we know enough from his correspondence, diaries and various anecdotes that have been recorded that he was a man given to extraordinary arrogance and pretentiousness—he bore all the traits and shortcomings of a man with a serious messiah complex. Nevertheless, Heidegger was irritated by the superficiality of the celebrity he enjoyed since he saw it as another symptom of the superficiality of the age and the growing tendency towards a kind of journalistic acquaintance with his philosophy as opposed to an earnest attempt to grapple with the complexity of the philosophical problems he had identified. There is an amusing episode which demonstrates how disarming Heidegger found his fame at times. Heidegger, who was now in his seventies, had been working on the proofs of some of his manuscripts in Freiburg with Heinrich Petzet. In the evening they adjourned to a local hostelry and were enjoying a drink together when Heidegger was approached by an American student.

> We were about to leave and were already standing at the exit of the restaurant when a young woman, obviously a student, approached Heidegger, mumbled a couple of words in embarrass-

ment, and handed him a piece of paper. Heidegger was no less embarrassed and looked at me helplessly. I had to laugh; I gave him my pen and told him he should give the young lady his autograph. While he stood there writing his name, I added, 'Please do not forget the date. This is important'. Radiating delight, the beautiful autograph-seeker bowed to the great man who had fulfilled her wish. Outside in the snow, Heidegger stood shaking his head and said, 'Such a thing!' This was indeed his first autograph in Freiburg. I commented, 'Yes, Herr Professor, when one is famous, such things happen'. Then he laughed. (Petzet, 1993, 185–86)[5]

Heidegger's childhood, from what we can gather, was unremarkable, with the exception of his academic prowess, which quickly became apparent. Heidegger was already earmarked by his instructors from a young age and was not just the precocious young student that we might expect to find in any classroom—there were concrete early indications of a truly remarkable intellect. One anecdote in particular bears retelling. On one occasion Heidegger was caught reading a copy of Kant's *Critique of Pure Reason* during a boring class and, recognising the extraordinary intellectual ambition of the teenage student, the principal of the school, Conrad Gröber,[6] subsequently presented Heidegger with a copy of a book which was to determine the entire trajectory of his philosophical career (see Gadamer 1994, 168). The book in question was Franz Brentano's 1862 dissertation *On the Manifold Meaning of Being According to Aristotle*[7]—a text that was to exercise a decisive influence on the young Heidegger and which he credited with setting him on the path to *Being and Time*. Indeed, for Heidegger, this particular event ignited his lifelong fascination with the question of being. There is a sense in which Heidegger's entire philosophical output, which already runs to over one hundred volumes in his ever expanding collected works (*Gesamtausgabe*), always comes back to this one question in some shape or form.

Since Heidegger's parents were not in a position to pay for a university education, the church was funding his studies; thus, when Heidegger first attended university it was to pursue studies in theology and philosophy. Heidegger's mother, in particular, was delighted by her brilliant young son's decision to pursue a vocation as a priest but was equally shocked and dismayed when Heidegger abandoned his vocation. He eventually broke his ties with the Catholic Church altogether. Heidegger famously presented his mother with a copy of *Being and Time* on her deathbed shortly after it was published in 1927.[8] He apparently considered it an act of atonement for disappointing his mother's previous hopes for her son. Heidegger had a younger sister and brother, and though neither of his siblings followed Heidegger's example by pursuing a career in academia, Heidegger's younger brother, Fritz, was close to Martin and often assisted him with his work—storing unpublished manuscripts and often aiding Heidegger in the correcting and transcription of his texts.[9] When Heidegger's health began to fail during his studies, he was deemed physically unfit for service in the church and, as mentioned previously, eventually abandoned his vocation altogether.[10] This was to be one of the first real crises in Heidegger's life and he spent an extended period of time at home, recuperating and fretting over how he was to pursue his university education without the support of the church. Heidegger essentially needed to secure enough funding to complete his graduate training. Eventually he did manage to cobble together the requisite funds from a variety of sources and was awarded a doctorate in philosophy in 1913. Heidegger now needed to work on his qualifying thesis, which would allow him to lecture.

Heidegger was, by this stage, in a relationship with Elfride Petri, whom he was to marry in 1917. Elfride appears to have been, in many ways, quite a progressive woman; she originally went into teaching but, feeling somewhat dissatisfied and stifled by this profession,[11] she went on to pursue further studies in economics at the University of Freiburg. Elfride had a reputation as a rather abrasive and bellicose character, and there are many anecdotes concerning her discourteous and abrupt behaviour toward people visiting Heidegger in Freiburg and Todtbauberg. Significantly, Elfride was fiercely nationalistic and a committed antisemite; indeed, she had a reputation for a virulent antisemitism which appears to have been more deep-seated, or certainly, more openly professed than that of her husband. As her granddaughter writes in her preface to Heidegger's letters to Elfride (which she edited),

> It was characteristic of [Elfride] that she objected to the non-German names we had chosen for our children. To the end of her days she did not essentially change in her nationalistic and antisemitic views. (LW, preface, x)

Heidegger himself was also fiercely nationalistic and remained committed to valourising a particular conception of German existence to which he was drawn as a son of the Swabian-Alemannic region. Heidegger further proved reluctant to relinquish many aspects of his disastrous attempts at a political philosophy and remained a critic of democracy and liberalism to the end of his days.[12] In an infamous interview with *Der Spiegel*, conducted in 1966 and published posthumously at his request in 1976, Heidegger confirmed again his enmity to democracy and his belief in the unique destiny of the German people and language and the importance of the German poet Holderlin's work to a renewal of Western spiritual life. When one considers the overtly political manner in which Heidegger began to turn to Hölderlin in his famous 1934 lectures at the University of Freiburg, one realises just how entrenched Heidegger's provincialism and nationalism were.

Heidegger had two sons, Jörg and Hermann, born in 1919 and 1920, respectively. What we did not know until relatively recently is that Martin was not, in fact, Hermann's father. Shortly after their marriage, Elfride had an affair with a childhood friend, Dr Friedel Caesar. She became pregnant and had a son, Hermann, in 1920. Heidegger appears to have accepted his wife's infidelity and agreed to raise Hermann as his own son. He even went so far as to ask the boy's biological father to be godfather to the child. Given Heidegger's lifelong litany of indiscretions and love affairs, one might be tempted to suppose that although Heidegger *appeared* to accept his own wife's indiscretion without recrimination or reproach, he ultimately spent the rest of his life exacting his revenge, over and over again. The recently published letters that Heidegger wrote to Elfride throughout their long relationship attest to a long-suffering wife who endured repeated infidelities by her husband, a man who also saw fit to abandon his family for extended periods to concentrate on his work and his extramarital affairs while his wife put his interests and concerns ahead of her own. Thus, their marriage might appear to have been remarkable in that raising the child of a wife's lover in the early 1920s would have been anything but conventional, and Heidegger initially *appeared* to have accepted the situation with commendable maturity and forbearance. However, Heidegger was to prove a less than faithful husband for the rest of his life until he suffered a stroke in his late seventies. His letters to Elfride make for sensational reading at times in that it is hard to imagine that this famous philosophical figure could have found the time to have quite so many extramarital affairs. Elfride, who was a difficult and curmudgeonly individual in her own right, was forced to endure many humiliations and indignities as a result of her husband's philandering over the years. Nevertheless, they appear to have lived out the last years of Martin's life in relative peace and harmony. One of the things that becomes clear from reading Heidegger's letters is just how selfish and narcissistic a person he could be, and his capacities for mendacity and denial are fathomless. He rarely seems to express anything even remotely close to genuine remorse for the pain and humiliation he subjected his wife to.

NOTES

1. Theodor Adorno was an influential German philosopher who died in 1969 at the age of sixty-five. Adorno is associated in particular with an intellectual movement in the twentieth century known as Critical Theory, which was inaugurated by a group of thinkers sometimes collectively referred to as 'The Frankfurt School'. Adorno had left Germany during the 1930s and was one of many German intellectual exiles in the United States during the Nazi regime. When Adorno returned to Germany he became one of the most vocal influences in German intellectual life. He was also one of Heidegger's harshest critics and was eager to dismantle Heidegger's philosophical influence and expose his philosophy of authenticity as symptomatic of a jargon of authenticity that had had a disastrous influence on German intellectual and cultural life. Adorno published a well-known book on this topic, *The Jargon of Authenticity*. It is typically read as a sustained polemic against Heidegger, even though it is a more generally oriented critique.

2. For an interesting discussion of the relevance of Heidegger's life to an understanding of his work, see Peter Trawny (2015, 64–65).

3. Todtnauberg is a German village in the Black Forest roughly eighteen miles from Freiburg. The region was noted for skiing and hiking but today has become famous due to Heidegger's association with the region. Thousands of visitors make the pilgrimage to the hut on the hillside where the Heidegger family spent many Summers and where Heidegger wrote much of the philosophy for which he became famous. Heidegger originally drafted the majority of *Being and Time* in a neighbour's house close to where Elfride commissioned the building of a small chalet which was to become Heidegger's spiritual and philosophical retreat for most of his adult life, until he was restricted to the family home in Freiburg in his old age.

4. It is remarkable that Petzet alludes to Heidegger's antisemitism here as though it was an entirely innocuous feature of the philosopher's mind-set. This is a problem that we will return to in later sections.

5. Petzet also recounts a somewhat bizarre story which demonstrates just how famous Heidegger had become: 'The growing fame and the ever-increasing number of visitors from around the world were sometimes annoying to Heidegger, although a strict family routine kept him enclosed and protected his working hours. I remember the rather amusing incident one Sunday afternoon when a South American family of many members requested permission to enter the house with the desire expressed stammeringly as "Seulement voir Monsieur Heidegger" (Only to see Mr. Heidegger). After receiving permission and inspecting the prodigy while bowing to him, they left without uttering a word' (Petzet, 1993, 188).

6. Gröber was appointed Archbishop of Freiburg in 1932.

7. Heidegger repeatedly credited this text with awakening his interest in the question concerning the meaning of being. Brentano had made a careful study

of Aristotle as a doctoral student and published his dissertation (which focused on the various meanings of being discussed by Aristotle) in 1862. Brentano was to become a key figure for continental philosophy and exercised a decisive influence over a number of intellectuals who studied with him and went on to become major intellectual figures in their own right. Edmund Husserl himself was profoundly influenced by Brentano, having studied under him, and Brentano is still credited with being one of the formative figures for the phenomenological movement.

8. Heidegger had, from the end of 1918 onwards, sundered all ties with the Catholic Church, writing to his friend (Father Engelbert Krebs) to explain his fundamental disagreement with the system of Catholicism.

9. Heinrich Petzet describes a likable and popular man who remained close to his famous older brother throughout his life: 'In his last decades, Heidegger's native Messkirch was personified for him entirely in his brother Fritz. . . . Upon entering the small, wood-planked house on Friedrich-Ebert-Strasse in Messkirch and being led into the room where the manuscripts almost reached the ceiling in one corner—manuscripts that, as Kommerell noted on his visit to Todtnauberg, were "all unpublished"—one could perhaps assume that these manuscripts were the intellectual treasures of Heidegger's brother Fritz. But Fritz only protected these manuscripts, prepared handwritten copies of them, and kept them in order. Nevertheless, his participation was important because the brothers used to discuss everything with each other, to weigh critical formulations and test each other's knowledge of the classics in Greek and Latin. We cannot imagine Heidegger's work without the assistance of his brother, who occasionally expressed contrary views but never presumed to take a stance against the philosopher. His whole life long, the latter was grateful to "his only brother" Fritz, who was younger and who survived Heidegger only four years. On 1 July 1980, Fritz was buried, with more than half of Messkirch and numerous friends of Heidegger's from all over Germany and even from France attending' (Petzet, 1993, 210–11).

10. Heidegger's condition proved not to be life-threatening, but it meant that he was later deemed fit for only limited military service during the First World War.

11. At the time a schoolteacher was one of the few professions that was available to women.

12. There is also fairly clear-cut evidence that Heidegger harboured views which simply must be characterised as antisemitic in nature, even if his views were not quite so repugnant as the rabid antisemitism which was a feature of everyday life in Nazi Germany.

THREE
Rumours of the Hidden King

Some confusion that has persisted in terms of Heidegger's intellectual development concerns the influence that Edmund Husserl's phenomenology exercised on the young philosopher. Granted, Heidegger did dedicate *Being and Time* to his former mentor and, to the end of his life, in public at least, professed his admiration for Husserl's phenomenological method, at least in one of its earlier incarnations, before the latter had devoted himself to his project of transcendental phenomenology. Heidegger himself needed to pay lip service to the idea that Husserl was his mentor and early guide. He had very clearly acted publicly towards Husserl in such a way as to give that impression in what was a carefully choreographed and calculated piece of manipulation designed to win the favour of one of the most important and influential philosophical voices in Germany at the time. However, when one considers Heidegger's private correspondence along with reports concerning his public repudiation of Husserl in his lectures in Marburg, it seems clear that by the time he was working on the ideas that were to evolve into *Being and Time*, he had become quite disenchanted with Husserl's mature project.[1] That is not to say that Heidegger had *never* been influenced by Husserl; after all, because he wanted to develop his understanding of Brentano's text and was aware of the fact that Husserl's philosophy was heavily influenced by Brentano, Heidegger decided to borrow Husserl's *Logical Investigations* from the university library; that text apparently sat on his desk throughout his student years. Heidegger discovered phenomenology as a result of this chance encounter, and by the time he was to get around to writing his qualifying thesis, 'Habilitationsschrift', some years later, it was clear that he had incorporated a lot of the vocabulary of phenomenology into his work. However, Heidegger's thought here goes very much against the grain of the insights that were to fuel the project of *Being and Time*. If anything, his breakthrough in the 1920s involves a radical break from this early influence of Husserl's transcendental phenomenology, and neo-Kantianism among other things.[2] In an interesting, if controversial, study of Heidegger's early philosophical work, John van Buren reminds the reader of Heidegger's self-understanding from the time of his qualifying dissertation: 'In the preface to the doctoral dissertation, Heidegger fittingly described himself as an "unhistorical mathematician"' (van Buren, 1994, 84). No characterisation could be further away from the Heidegger that introduces *Being and Time* to the world. As van Buren memorably notes in his text,

> After completing his two dissertations, all the poetry, mysticism, hermeneutics, Dilthey, Kierkegaard, Nietzsche, and who knows what else that the young logician and Neo-Scholastic had been reading started to catch up with him. The philosophical tension between timelessly valid sense and spatiotemporal reality was at this time also a tension within Heidegger's own philosophical personality—and it would soon snap. His phenomenological suspension (*Ausschalten*) of the flux of spatiotemporal reality was also a suppression of his own philosophical impulses. *Ausschalten* ordinarily means 'turning off' something—the water or the electricity, for example. Between 1915 and 1919, the damning up of Heidegger's philosophical and religious impulses finally burst, and we have been trying to cope with this explosion ever since. (van Buren, 1994, 88)

Van Buren goes on to write,

> After giving up his theological studies, Heidegger had tried his best to become a Neo-Scholastic, a mathematician, a phenomenological neo-Kantian, a pure logician, but it was not in him. Instead, after 1915 he turned into Heidegger the young romantic and passionate rebel who advocated a fundamental critique of his own metaphysical heritage and a revolution to a new postmetaphysical beginning. (van Buren, 1994, 89)

It was during the 1920s, first as a *Privatdozent* in Freiburg and then, especially as a lecturer in Marburg,[3] that Heidegger really began to formulate the ideas and themes that were to develop into one of the most influential and important philosophical texts of the twentieth century: *Being and Time*. And there can be no denying that during this period, Heidegger had moved away in important respects from Husserlian phenomenology and neo-Kantianism and, thus, his own earlier 'unhistorical' efforts. In recent years, considerable attention has been paid to Heidegger's lecture courses in Marburg during the early to mid-1920s, when his ideas would have been gestating. It was during this period in particular that Heidegger recognised the importance of time as history for the philosophical project he wished to inaugurate.

If Heidegger's earlier philosophical efforts had been attempts to formulate absolute truths and principles grounded firmly in mathematics and logic, and had been influenced by philosophies that relied on such firmly grounded principles, his work in the 1920s began to reflect a growing dissatisfaction with the notion of an absolutely a priori philosophy conceived in an ahistorical vacuum. Heidegger had always been drawn to German literature and poetry—he was heavily influenced by the Romantic movement while the insights of a range of thinkers began to weave their way into Heidegger's thinking. He began to realise the importance of time understood as history for the manner in which human beings come to understand themselves and the world around them. During this period, Heidegger begins to subject the transcendental character of Husserl's mature project to severe criticism along with what he takes to be the dry, anaemic formalism of the neo-Kantians that was so prevalent in Germany at the time. Heidegger begins simultaneously to work on the notion of a hermeneutics of facticity[4] and stresses the importance of the affective while devoting considerable attention to the practical philosophy of Aristotle and Augustine's *Confessions*. He delivers lectures on the concept of time and begins to formulate his own account of temporality.

Throughout the 1920s, Heidegger was developing the ideas and themes which were to eventually form the basis for *Being and Time*. In his Marburg period, Heidegger began to *openly* distance himself from the transcendental phenomenology of Husserl and to focus instead on the role that time and temporality plays within his analyses of factical life. Rumours of Heidegger's derogatory remarks and jaundiced attitude towards Husserl's work began to make their way back to his mentor, who had been tirelessly championing his protégé's cause for some time. Heidegger reassured Husserl that these were malicious rumours, nothing more than idle gossip and reaffirmed his admiration and support for Husserl's phenomenology.

However, in Heidegger's less guarded moments, he was indeed openly hostile to Husserl's work and made no secret of his opposition to Husserl in his correspondence with Jaspers, for example. Indeed, once Heidegger's academic future was made secure with his appointment to a permanent post in Marburg, he quickly began to declare to Jaspers that he would now begin to speak 'openly' and that people would begin to see, hear and read what he really believed philosophically.

In his biography of Heidegger, Rüdiger Safranski quotes from Heidegger's correspondence with Jaspers during this period. He explains that while 'publicly Heidegger still describes Husserl as his teacher, and although he benefits from his support, he has already distanced himself from him so far that, in a letter to Jaspers, he includes him among the blasphemed medicine men'. Safranski goes on to quote from one of Heidegger's letters to Jaspers:

> No doubt you know that Husserl has an invitation to Berlin; he behaves worse than a *Privatdozent* who confuses a professorship with eternal bliss. . . . Husserl has totally gone to pieces—if indeed he ever was in one piece—which I have been increasingly questioning—he vacillates this way and that and utters trivialities such as would reduce one to tears. He lives by his mission of being 'the founder of phenomenology', no one has any idea what that is—anyone who has been here for a semester realises what's happening—he is beginning to suspect that the people are no longer following him. . . . And such a person today hopes to save the world in Berlin. (Safranski, 1998, 128)

It was also during this period that the relatively unknown young lecturer met Hannah Arendt and began a passionate love affair that was to have profound consequences for both of their lives right up until Arendt's death in 1975. She had come to Marburg in 1924 at the age of eighteen and began attending Heidegger's lectures. Although Heidegger was still very much an unestablished philosophical figure in the German academic scene, Arendt, Hans-Georg Gadamer, Karl Löwith, Jacob Klein, Leo Strauss and a number of Heidegger's other students from that period have all confirmed that rumours were beginning to spread of this eccentric young lecturer's brilliance and magnetic personality in the lecture hall:

> Heidegger's 'fame' predates by about eight years the publication of *Sein und Zeit* (*Being and Time*) in 1927; indeed it is open to question whether the unusual success of this book—not just the immediate impact it had inside and outside the academic world

but also its extraordinary lasting influence, with which few of the century's publications can compare—would have been possible if it had not been preceded by the teacher's reputation among the students, in whose opinion, at any rate, the book's success merely confirmed what they had known for many years . . . in Heidegger's case there was nothing tangible on which his fame could have been based, nothing written, save for notes taken at his lectures which circulated among students everywhere. These lectures dealt with texts that were generally familiar; they contained no doctrine that could have been learned, reproduced, and handed on. There was hardly more than a name, but the name travelled all over Germany like the rumor of the hidden king. (Arendt, 1971, 1)

Commentators on the relationship between Heidegger and Arendt have been rather jaundiced against Heidegger, and their accounts usually depict the young Arendt as a helpless victim of a manipulative, narcissistic, academic predator. In most of these cases, the same critics are Arendt specialists, have no real grasp of Heidegger's work, and come to their projects with their minds very much already made up on the matter of their romantic involvement. For example, in a somewhat less than even-handed account, Elzbieta Ettinger reports on how Heidegger offered a number of reasons as to why it would behove Arendt to leave Marburg to pursue her studies elsewhere rather than remaining there to continue her studies under Heidegger:

> Nor, he said, is it especially beneficial to be regarded as a 'Heidegger student'—a bizarre statement coming from a philosopher who had no equal in Germany. (Ettinger, 1995, 21)

This is terribly tendentious, however; in effect, this is to retrospectively attribute to Heidegger a status and rank in the German academy which he simply *did not possess* at that time. It is also worth recalling that Heidegger was very much a figure who divided opinion in established German philosophical circles. He had also been passed over in favour of other philosophers for jobs which he had pinned his hopes on and had suffered a number of disappointments and setbacks before managing to secure a permanent post in Marburg. It would not have been entirely unreasonable to advise Arendt to establish philosophical links with other philosophers, then. Of course, one must acknowledge that Heidegger had selfish motives as well, and he certainly cannot be cast in a favourable light on this issue. He was a married man with children and had embarked on a clandestine affair with a teenage student, using all of his considerable charm and charisma as a brilliant young philosopher to do so. However, we should credit Arendt with a little more autonomy in this matter; she was a strong, brilliant young intellectual, fiercely independent and brave. Arendt and Heidegger fell in love, and, as with many people who find themselves in that particular predicament, they struggled to cope with their situation when life and Heidegger's own commitments to his wife and family began to get in their way. Heidegger clearly did not always conduct himself as he should have; however, in this instance at least, there appears to have been a genuine and abiding passionate bond between the two that never entirely dissipated. Moreover, it seems rather condescending to characterise one of the most prominent and courageous intellectual figures of the twentieth century as a helpless little schoolgirl.

NOTES

1. Heidegger appears to have been more impressed with Husserl's earlier philosophical efforts which did not, for Heidegger, have the same transcendental baggage as the 'later' Husserl. Heidegger was quite critical of Husserl's later attempts to perform a kind of bracketing (*epoche*) of everything that we might normally class as our everyday experience and beliefs. Husserl calls this the suspension of the natural attitude and it involves bracketing everything except what he takes to be indubitable in terms of the flow of conscious experience. What is left over includes the transcendental ego, the forms of time consciousness that make sense of how we experience anything (retention and protention), along with the intentional structure of all conscious experience. For Heidegger, then, Husserl's later project involved an unwarranted abstraction and bracketing of the world of our everyday experience which led his inquiries astray.

2. Neo-Kantianism was an influential philosophical movement in Germany in the late nineteenth and early twentieth century. Heidegger himself was influenced by a number of neo-Kantian philosophers, notably Heinrich Rickert and Paul Natorp. He participated in a famous public debate with another leading neo-Kantian philosopher of the day, Ernst Cassirer, in 1929 at Davos. The neo-Kantians, as the name suggests, favoured a revitalisation of a Kantian approach to philosophy, challenging the dominant approaches of the day. Their rallying cry was 'back to Kant'. Husserl conceives of phenomenology as a challenge, in some respects, to the neo-Kantians; thus, his famous slogan becomes 'back to the things themselves'. One might suppose here that the reference is to the Kantian 'thing-in-itself'. However, for the phenomenologist, the 'things' are appearances, that is, the phenomena.

3. Heidegger was appointed to the position of Extraordinary Professor at the University of Marburg in 1923.

4. Heidegger was keen to use hermeneutics as part of his philosophical approach to the question concerning the meaning of being. Hermeneutics is derived from the Greek *hermeneuein*, which means 'to interpret'. In the seven-

teenth century, hermeneutics was explicitly identified as a theory of interpretation and a crucial tool for analysing and understanding religious texts, legal texts and ancient literature. As we shall see in the discussion of *Being and Time*, Heidegger proposes to undertake a hermeneutics of facticity. Again, the term facticity is related to 'fact' (though not in the sense of a brute fact, or simple matter of fact), and Heidegger had been interested in the notion of our factical or everyday existence as the appropriate site from which to launch an investigation into the meaning of being as he was convinced that our everyday life was already saturated with a pre-theoretical sense of being to begin which. There is a whole series of facts about our situated existence over which we have no control and that are part of the context within which we understand ourselves before we begin to theorise or abstract. In his analysis of our everyday existence, Heidegger sifts his way through the pre-theoretical, sedimented layers of that meaning.

FOUR
The Hidden King Returns to Freiburg

The publication of *Being and Time* in 1927 quickly established Heidegger as one of the most recognisable and important philosophers of his era. The impact of this extraordinary book was immediate and seismic, irrevocably changing the course of twentieth and, now, twenty-first century philosophy. It is a book that has lost none of its original force, influencing generation after generation of philosophers. Emmanuel Levinas, who studied for a time in Freiburg under both Heidegger and Husserl and who was to become a resolute critic of Heidegger's philosophy, insisted to the end of his life that *Being and Time* stood out as one of the major texts in the Western philosophical tradition.

> I became enchanted with Heidegger and his *Being and Time,* and I still think very highly of it: there are only five or six books like this in the history of philosophy.[1]

Heidegger had published relatively little to that point and, even though the English translation of *Being and Time* runs to almost six hundred pages, the book was essentially the first two of three divisions of Part I of a two-part project which was rushed to publication. Heidegger was being considered for the chair in Marburg vacated by Nicolai Hartmann and was under intense pressure to publish a substantial piece of written work.[2] Despite the haste with which Heidegger pulled the text together, *Being and Time* is regarded as one of the most important philosophical works of the twentieth century. One might wonder what became of the other sections of the much larger project which Heidegger had originally planned. The answer to that question is complicated and contentious. Indeed, this is one of the main issues over which opposing Heidegger scholars launch their interpretive campaigns against one another, that is, on the issue of the 'turn' in Heidegger's thought. Some opponents of the idea that Heidegger 'turned' away from the project of *Being and Time* try to show how, in many respects, Heidegger is trying to complete the project initially outlined in the original blueprints of the overarching project of *Being and Time*. Their adversaries, conversely, refuse to acknowledge any such consistency between the early and late Heidegger. I am inclined toward the view that there is something to the position of the former camp, though that position is certainly overstated as things stand. With respect to the latter camp, their positions are typically based on a particular interpretive move: these scholars often conflate the notion of a 'turn' (*die Kehre*) with the change or shift in approach and language we begin to see in the decades following the publication of *Being and Time* and thus suppose that this evolving and changing language represents a 'reversal', a 'turning away from' and thus a repudiation of Heidegger's early masterpiece. These kinds of interpretations, it seems to me, often ignore or suppress the evolving and continuous nature of Heidegger's philosophical development. Notwithstanding, this is a hotly contested issue in Heidegger studies and one that does not look like it will be resolved any time soon.

Being and Time is unquestionably Heidegger's most famous book and by far and away his most important publication. He himself returned to it again and again, invoking it repeatedly by way of explaining key developments in his later thought. Although Heidegger's prose becomes notoriously obscure and complex following *Being and Time*, people still struggle to come to grips with Heidegger's unique idiom even in this early text. That is not to say that Heidegger had effectively finished everything he wanted to say by 1927; however, there is something to the idea that Heidegger never fully relinquishes some of the key ideas that he was developing in *Being and Time*. Of course, Heidegger's views evolve and develop, and a number of Heideggerians rightly underline the importance of some of his later work, which doesn't simply reduce to an elaboration of some passage or other in *Being and Time*. Notwithstanding, and as I mentioned at the outset, this is an introduction which favours a continuity thesis over the alternative approach, but it is not a debate which we can hope to engage with properly here. I should also remind the reader that all we can hope to offer here is a brief introduction to some of the key ideas in Heidegger's work. There are any number of detailed and comprehensive commentaries on this difficult text which offer rigorous analysis and exegesis for readers who wish to delve deeper into *Being and Time*.

BEING AND TIME

As one may have guessed from the title alone, the central preoccupation of Heidegger's masterpiece is 'being', and Heidegger will suggest that time is central to the question of the meaning of being. Heidegger is interested, then, in the question concerning the *meaning* of being. What do we mean by this word, 'being'? On the very first page, Heidegger quotes from Plato's *Sophist*, a dialogue to which he had devoted an important lecture course in the mid-1920s: 'For manifestly you have long been aware of what you mean when you use the expression "*being*". We, however, who used to think we understood it, have now become perplexed'. Heidegger goes on to pose a question of his own, a question which was to fuel his lifelong philosophical efforts:

> Do we in our time have an answer to the question of **what we really mean by the word 'being'?** Not at all. So it is fitting that we should raise anew *the question of the **meaning of Being**.* But are we nowadays even perplexed at our inability to understand the expression 'Being'? Not at all. So first of all we must reawaken an understanding for the meaning of the question. Our aim in the following treatise is to work out the question of the meaning of *Being* and to do so concretely. Our provisional aim is the Interpretation of *time* as the possible horizon for any understanding whatsoever of Being. (BT, 1; emphasis added)

As was mentioned briefly, as a teenager, Heidegger had already become fascinated with the question of being as a result of his study of Brentano's book on Aristotle. It is hardly an overstatement to say that the being-question became the guiding one for all of his subsequent work. Heidegger believes that the question of being animated the titanic efforts of Plato and Aristotle. Later he will credit the Presocratics with major insights here as well, but he also insists that part of what was vital in their thinking has become trivialised and obscured—obscured to such an extent in fact that, today, the notion or concept of being itself is dismissed as 'the most universal and emptiest of concepts', one that is, as a result, beyond definition. Not only that, it enjoys unproblematic currency on a daily basis: people use the word 'being' and its verbal inflections—is, are, were—so readily and constantly as to suggest that being does not need any further clarification or analysis. Suffice it to say that Heidegger believes that this is a sorry philosophical state of affairs and one which has had dire consequences, not just for philosophy, but for humanity itself. Indeed, he will eventually go so far as to suggest that the salvation of the planet from the reigning crisis of 'unchained technology' depends on something like the mission of retrieval that his philosophy embarks on.

It can sometimes be difficult for those unacquainted with Heidegger's work to get a handle on where he is coming from in terms of his reasons for approaching the being-question in the way that he does in *Being and Time*. One of the issues that tends to cloud people's understanding of the text is what appears to be an emphasis on human existence or the human condition per se. However, Heidegger is really looking at the question concerning the *meaning* of *being*. He is already convinced that there is a kind of privileging of presence at work in our sense of what being means which distorts the nature of reality for us and indeed our own self-understanding. Heidegger is convinced that the history of Western metaphysics is dominated by a tendency to privilege presence and to ignore or suppress the absence which is the constant concomitant of any sense of presence. This in part explains Heidegger's efforts to underline the importance of absence or nothingness in some of his texts from the late 1920s and 1930s. Part of what Heidegger begins to challenge is the idea that whenever we use the word being (or 'is', 'are' 'were', etc.) that what we mean is that something exists or is present. Heidegger wants to show that we often use the verb 'to be' in ways that denote more than something being simply 'present'. This is something that he believes has become progressively more obscured in the Western tradition at least going as far back as Plato and Aristotle.

Introduction to Metaphysics was the first of Heidegger's lecture courses that he chose to publish, appearing in 1953, some eighteen years after he had held the course in Freiburg. In the preface to the seventh edition of *Being and Time*, Heidegger recommends the work as a companion piece to *Being and Time*. This was to become a strategy of Heidegger as he began to pair certain lecture courses with other published works that might initially be less accessible than a lecture course specifically aimed at students. Before turning to *Being and Time* directly, then, we will try to piggyback Heidegger's efforts to introduce to his own students in 1935 some of the basic ideas that he was grappling with when he was working on *Being and Time*.

Heidegger begins with Leibniz's famous question:

> Why are there beings at all instead of nothing? That is the question . . . this is obviously the first of all questions. Of course, it is not the first question in the chronological sense. Individuals as well as peoples ask many questions in the course of their historical passage through time. They explore, investigate, and test many sorts of things before they run into the question 'Why are there beings at all instead of nothing?' Many never run into this question at all, if running into the question means not only hearing and reading the interrogative sentence as uttered, but asking the question, that is, taking a stand on it, posing it, compelling oneself into the state of this questioning.
>
> And yet, we are each touched once, maybe even now and then, by the concealed power of this question, without properly grasping what is happening to us. In great despair, for example, when all weight tends to dwindle away from things and the sense of things grows dark, the question looms. Perhaps it strikes only once, like the muffled tolling of a bell that resounds into Dasein and gradually fades away. The question is there in heartfelt joy, for then all things are transformed and surround us as if for the first time, as if it were easier to grasp that they were not, rather than that they are, and are as they are. The question is there in a spell of boredom, when we are equally distant from despair and joy, but when the stubborn ordinariness of beings lays open a wasteland in which it makes no difference to us whether beings are or are not—and then, in a distinctive form, the question resonates once again: Why are there beings at all instead of nothing? (IM, 1–2)

There is a sense, then, that this is the broadest, most fundamental question in metaphysics; it is first in rank and comes before all other questions in terms of depth and scope—nothing exceeds or escapes its range, not even the notion of nothing itself, precisely because it 'is' nothing and thus is related to the question of being. But, as Heidegger will begin to draw out in the course of the opening lectures, when we pose this question of being and non-being or nothing, do we have an adequate sense of 'being'? What do we mean by this word 'being'—what does this verb so commonly invoked bring to the party? Of course, the obvious answer is 'presence' or 'existence' and, for this reason, Leibniz's own question focuses on the simple issue of presence versus absence, that is, being versus nothingness. As Heidegger says in one of the later reflections on his famous inaugural lecture, 'What Is Metaphysics?'

> Is it perhaps from this that the as yet unshaken presumption has entered all metaphysics that an understanding of 'Being' may simply be taken for granted and that the Nothing can therefore be dealt with more easily than beings? That is indeed the situation regarding Being and Nothing. If it were different, then Leibniz could not have said in the same place by way of an explanation: 'Car le rien est plus simple et plus facile que quelque chose [For the nothing is simpler and easier than any thing]'. (Introduction to 'What Is Metaphysics?' PM, 190)

Heidegger notes something that he considers both non-trivial and which he thinks the tradition has not adequately addressed. We say of many things that they 'are' in various ways when it is not clear that that means that they exist as fully *present* or actualised before us. For example, if I say that I see a clearing in the forest, or a gap in the hedge, I say that there 'is' a gap. But what does it mean to say that there is a 'gap', literally an absence of trees in one instance or foliage on the side of the road on the other? Someone might try to counter that this is just a trick of language, that all we mean is that there is a space where no trees are growing or no hedge is growing. But think of how else we might express this—'there *are* no trees in that part of the forest' or 'there *is nothing* between those two pieces of hedge'. What do we mean with these inflections, 'are' and 'is', of the verb 'being'? What does the term itself actually *mean*? One might be tempted to go the route of first order logic here and suggest that if we rewrite the sentences using existential quantifiers, then this kind of problem dissolves. Heidegger would most likely counter that that is because the logician has already assumed that being means presence (understood here as continuous presence) and that any talk of 'the nothing' as somehow 'being' is literally nonsense. The logician might try to rewrite a similar kind of sentence by translating it into other sentences that appear to have the same meaning, which can, in turn, be translated using existential quantifiers. Under something like this formulation, one might say that there is no problem at all and that, in an ideal language, one does not have to posit the presence of absence in order to understand the statement that there is a gap or clearing in the forest. However, Heidegger is unsatisfied with this kind of approach. He anticipates it and rejects it in his *Introduction to Metaphysics* as well as in his 1940s' retrospectives on his 1929 essay, 'What Is Metaphysics?', which was famously attacked by Rudolf Carnap in a 1932 paper.³

As Heidegger writes in his 1949 introduction to 'What Is Metaphysics?',

> If, as we unfold the question concerning the truth of Being, we speak of overcoming metaphysics, this means: recalling Being itself. Such recalling goes beyond the traditional failure to think the ground of the root of philosophy. The thinking attempted in *Being and Time* sets out on the way to prepare an overcoming of metaphysics, so understood. (PM, 279)

In a 1943 'Postscript to "What Is Metaphysics?"' Heidegger suggests that his basic question 'springs from a thinking that has already entered into the overcoming of metaphysics' (PM, 231). Heidegger further argues that any such attempts to overcome 'must continue to speak the language of that which they help overcome' (PM, 231). Heidegger fulminates against the idea of a presuppositionless inquiry, suggesting instead that we begin from the presuppositions that we already operate with before abstracting and then consider the basic meaning or understanding of things we have before we inquire further.⁴ Furthermore, Heidegger, in returning to some of the key ideas animating *Being and Time*, while reassessing a lecture first delivered two years after he published that text, reminds his readers that his key question is related to the Leibnizian question, why are there beings at all instead of nothing? As we mentioned earlier, he famously revisits the Leibnizian question in *Introduction to Metaphysics*, identifying it as the fundamental question for Western metaphysics. He has by now diagnosed this as a metaphysics of presence, a metaphysics that he wants to overcome, because it misrepresents the way we actually experience and perceive. As he writes in another 1940s' retrospective on the 1929 lecture:

> Metaphysics does not ask this question [the being-question, the *Seinsfrage*] because it thinks Being only by representing being as beings. It means beings as a whole, although it speaks of Being. It names Being and means beings as beings. From its beginning to its completion, the propositions of metaphysics have been strangely involved in a persistent confusion of beings and Being. (PM, 281)

In the 1929 lecture, Heidegger anticipates much of what he will discuss in his famous 1935 lecture course concerning the question of the nothing and the related ways that he attempts to put pressure on the tradition. He dismisses again what he takes to be stock objections which rely on the principle of non-contradiction, since that approach, for Heidegger, has already conflated being with presence and has made a decision about the meaning of being, unwitting or otherwise, which he wishes to call into question.

For Heidegger, then, the 'nothing' is dismissed as a result of a fateful prejudice concerning the meaning of being which has dominated Western thought. Being has, since that time, been discussed always and everywhere in terms of beings and, thus, as reducing always and everywhere to 'presence', that is, constant, static presence. In the series of texts I have mentioned, when discussing the notion of 'nothing', Heidegger both explicitly and implicitly targets the principle of non-contradiction. The principle of non-contradiction then is routinely invoked to dismiss all talk of the nothing as simply wrong-headed, illogical, unscientific, in short, as contradictory. After all, to talk of nothing as 'being' in any way is to treat it as a present 'thing', to treat it as 'something' which is, of course, contradictory. But again, for Heidegger, this is already to have decided in advance that being reduces to presence, that it *is* present, or that it is itself *a* being and not nothing.

In the 1929 lecture, when his sights are set squarely on the role of nothingness, Heidegger briefly discusses his *Being and Time* account of our bare affective states—that is, the bare moods which all of our experience presupposes and which themselves attest to the way we find ourselves already thrown open as a site for the interplay of presence and absence. Part of what we are held out into, even in this early account in *Being and Time*, is the nothing, and Heidegger returns to and defends this idea in 1929, in 1935 and again in his 1940s' introduction and postscript to the 1929 lecture. Once again, this seems to invite us to think of *Being and Time* as anticipating the continuing attempts to resist the metaphysics of presence over the course of the rest of Heidegger's career.

It is worth bearing in mind here that Heidegger had some training in mathematics and logic[5] and, as we mentioned previously, that he described himself as an 'ahistorical mathematician' before his breakthroughs in the 1920s. So this is not the ill-informed prejudice of some literary crank with no real facility for mathematics or logic. In his 1935 lecture course, in order to illustrate his point with respect to the role of the nothing in terms of what it means for anything 'to be', Heidegger takes an immediate example from the lecture hall—a piece of chalk:

> The piece of chalk here is an extended, relatively stable, definitely formed, grayish-white thing, and furthermore, a thing for writing. As certainly as it belongs precisely to this thing to lie here, the capacity not to be here and not to be so big also belongs to it. The possibility of being drawn along the blackboard and used up is not something that we merely add onto the thing with our thought. The chalk itself, as this being, *is* in this possibility; otherwise it would not be chalk as a writing implement. Every being, in turn, has this Possible in it, in a different way in each case. This possible belongs to the chalk. (IM, 32)

In other words, what the chalk means, what we take it to mean when we say that the chalk 'is' in various ways, *means* more than simply stating that the chalk is 'present'. Of course it *is* present in various ways, but it can also be understood in all manner of *possible* ways that involve more than what is merely present at any given moment, ways that *could* be actualised, but *are* not yet. Moreover, this is a fundamental part of what it *means* for things to *be*. For Heidegger, the logician will be tempted to respond that when anyone says of the chalk that 'the chalk is', that this is adequately represented by the propositional form $\exists x C x$: there exists some entity/x such that that entity/x is a piece of chalk. Heidegger very clearly has Carnap and the logical positivists in mind here and explicitly targets the principle of non-contradiction:

> Whoever talks about Nothing does not know what he is doing. In speaking about Nothing, he makes it into a something. By speaking this way, he speaks against what he means. He contra-dicts himself. But self-contradictory speech is an offense against the fundamental rule of speech (*logos*), against 'logic'. Talking about Nothing is illogical. Whoever talks and thinks illogically is an unscientific person. Now whoever goes so far as to talk about Nothing within philosophy, which after all is the home of logic, deserves all the more to be accused of offending against the fundamental rule of all thinking. Such talk about Nothing consists in utterly senseless propositions. Moreover, whoever takes Nothing seriously takes the side of nullity. He obviously promotes the spirit of negation and serves disintegration. Talking about Nothing is not only completely contrary to thought, but it undermines all culture and faith. Whatever both disregards the fundamental law of thinking and also destroys faith and the will to construct is pure nihilism. (IM, 25–26)

The obvious suggestion here is that one should simply ignore the question or issue of the nothing. However, Heidegger notes that we already began with this question as a question that we received from the tradition, and he further notes that the question of being was always posed in conjunction with the question of nothingness from that same tradition.

> Our introduction of talk about Nothing here is not a careless and overly enthusiastic manner of speaking, nor our own invention, but merely strict respect for the originary tradition regarding the sense of the fundamental question. (IM, 26)

And yet, as Heidegger suggests, it may well be the case that the belief that this notion of 'Nothing' or any discussion of it is tantamount to nihilism, or a confounding of the fundamental and immutable laws of thinking rests 'on a misunderstanding'. And, for Heidegger, this misunderstanding is not arbitrary or incidental; it is the fundamental misapprehension that has governed the trajectory of Western thought since the time of the ancient Greeks:

> Of course, the misunderstanding that is being played out here is not accidental. Its ground is a lack of understanding that has long ruled the question about beings. But this lack of understanding stems from an *oblivion of Being* that is getting increasingly rigid. (IM, 27)

Heidegger is revisiting here some of the fundamental ideas motivating *Being and Time* in an effort to unpack them for his students. He reiterates his opposition to the idea that rules of logic such as the principle of non-contradiction necessarily operate as the rules upon which any understanding of anything whatsoever must be based, since this thinking itself rests upon a misunderstanding when it comes to the being-question.

> For it cannot be decided so readily whether logic and its fundamental rules can provide any measure for the question about beings as such. It could be the other way around, that the whole logic that we know and that we treat like a gift from heaven is grounded in a very definite answer to the question about beings, and that consequently any thinking that simply follows the laws of thought of established logic is intrinsically incapable of even beginning to understand the question about beings, much less of actually unfolding it and leading toward an answer. In truth, it is only an illusion of rigor and scientificity when one appeals to the principle of contradiction, and to logic in general, in order to prove that all thinking and all talk about Nothing is contradictory and therefore senseless. 'Logic' is then taken as a tribunal, secure for all eternity, and it goes without saying that no rational

human being will call into doubt its authority as the first and last court of appeal. Whoever speaks against logic is suspected, implicitly or explicitly, of arbitrariness. The mere suspicion already counts as an argument and an objection, and one takes oneself to be exempted from further, authentic reflection. (IM, 27)

Notwithstanding, Heidegger notes that one cannot discuss the notion of nothingness as if it itself were a thing, and therefore the notion of the nothing is not something which science, for example, can discuss. A thinking that is not scientific, in the traditional sense, is required. Not only that:

> All scientific thinking is just a rigidified form of philosophical thinking. Philosophy never arises from or through science. (IM, 29)

Heidegger calls the sciences into question and makes it quite clear that his philosophical inquiry is not operating in the same mode as that kind of inquiry and wants to see whether this notion of the nothing as something that is juxtaposed with being in the question he began with is really just 'a turn of phrase that says nothing and is arbitrarily appended, or whether even in the preliminary expression of the question it has an essential sense' (IM, 29). So, the question of nothingness has always, in our philosophical tradition, gone hand in hand with the question of being. We normally begin with 'beings' and, beings of course 'are'.

> They are given to us, they are in front of us and can thus be found before us at any time, and are also known to us within certain domains. Now the beings given to us in this way are immediately interrogated as to their ground. The question advances directly toward a ground. Such a method just broadens and enlarges, as it were, a procedure that is practised every day. Somewhere in the vineyard, for example, an infestation turns up, something indisputably present at hand. One asks: where does this come from, where and what is its ground? Similarly, as a whole, beings are present at hand. One asks: where and what is the ground? This kind of questioning is represented in the simple formula: Why are there beings? Where and what is their ground? Tacitly one is asking after another, higher being. But there the question does not pertain at all to beings as a whole and as such. (IM, 30)

One can see then that Heidegger is trying to identify a misstep that we have commonly taken when it comes to thinking about being and beings. We begin with things that are there for us and immediately begin to wonder as to *why* they are there, what is the cause of these beings. And traditionally—one closed off that line of questioning with the idea of a higher being that caused all the other beings. But this misses something for Heidegger since it glosses over the question as to what we mean by 'being' and simply asks for the cause (the why) of things that are present. This is to assume that what 'being' means when we say that beings 'are' reduces to 'presence'—that is, 'existent', and thus we have taken for granted precisely the issues that Heidegger thinks are open to further questioning. If one considers the original question again—'why are there beings at all instead of nothing?'—we notice now that one cannot accept the prejudice concerning logic and non-contradiction since we cannot in this case simply take beings as given in the first place according to the scope of this fundamental question. Rather we have to consider the possibility of there not being beings. The addition of the nothing to our question in this instance

> [p]revents us, in our questioning, from beginning directly with beings as unquestionably given, and having already begun, already moving on to the ground we are seeking which is also in being. Instead, these beings are held out in a questioning manner into the possibility of not-Being. In this way, the Why gains a completely different power and urgency of questioning. Why are beings torn from the possibility of not-Being? Why do they not fall back into it constantly with no further ado? Beings are now no longer what just happens to be present at hand; they begin to waver, regardless of whether we know beings with all certainty, regardless of whether we grasp them in their full scope or not. From now on, beings as such waver, insofar as we put them into the most extreme and sharpest counterpossibility of beings, into not-Being and Nothing. The search for the Why now transforms itself accordingly. It does not just try to provide a present-at-hand ground for explaining what is present at hand—instead, we are now searching for a ground that is supposed to ground the dominance of beings as an overcoming of Nothing. The ground in question is now questioned as the ground of the decision for beings over against Nothing—more precisely, as the ground for the wavering of the beings that sustain us and unbind us, half in being, half not in being, which is also why we cannot wholly belong to any thing, not even, to ourselves; yet Dasein is in each case mine. . . . Thus it is already becoming clearer that this 'instead of nothing?' is no superfluous addition to the real question. Instead, this turn of phrase is an essential component of the whole interrogative sentence, which as a whole expresses a com-

pletely different question from what is meant by the question: Why are there beings? With our question we establish ourselves among beings in such a way that they forfeit their self-evidence *as beings*. Insofar as beings come to waver within the broadest and harshest possibility of oscillation—the 'either beings—or nothing'—the questioning itself loses every secure foothold. Our Dasein, too, as it questions comes into suspense, and nevertheless maintains itself, by itself, in this suspense.

But beings are not changed by our questioning. They remain what they are and as they are. After all, our questioning is just a psychospiritual process in us that, however it may play itself out, cannot concern beings themselves. Certainly, beings remain as they are revealed to us. And yet beings are not able to shrug off what is worthy of questioning: they, as what they are and how they are, could also *not* be. By no means do we experience this possibility as something that is just added on by our own thought, but beings themselves declare this possibility [as part of how they appear to us], they declare themselves as being in this possibility. Our questioning just opens up the domain so that beings can break open in such questionworthiness. (IM, 30–32)[6]

Heidegger is trying to show that traditional approaches miss out on all of the possibilities inherent in what we 'mean' when we say that a piece of chalk, for example, *is* here, or there, or *is* something or other. Part of what it means for the chalk to be a particular piece of chalk is its possibility of being used up when drawn along the blackboard and thus to no longer be—this is part of what it means for the chalk to be: it 'is' in this possibility. But, Heidegger goes on to argue:

> Of course, when we look for this Possible in the chalk, we are accustomed and inclined to say that we do not see it and do not grasp it. But that is a prejudice. The elimination of this prejudice is part of the unfolding of our question. For now, this question should just open up beings, in their wavering between not-Being and Being. Insofar as beings stand up against the extreme possibility of not-Being, they themselves stand in Being, and yet they have never thereby overtaken and overcome the possibility of not-Being. (IM, 32–33)

Heidegger goes on to ask:

> How are we even supposed to inquire into the ground for the Being of beings, let alone be able to find it out, if we have not adequately conceived, understood and grasped Being itself? This enterprise would be just as hopeless as if someone wanted to

explain the cause and ground of a fire and declared that he need not bother with the course of the fire or the investigation of its scene.

So it turns out that the question 'Why are there beings at all instead of nothing?' forces us to the prior question: '*How does it stand with Being?*' (IM, 34)

Heidegger is convinced that there is a fundamental problem which has persistently led philosophy astray. In short, the Western tradition has taken the meaning of being itself to be self-evident and has thus overlooked an important philosophical dimension to the way things become meaningful for us and how we in turn project meanings onto the world around us. Without getting too far ahead of ourselves, Heidegger believes that we have inherited a philosophical tradition, which, for all its variety, vagaries and conflicting views, is based on an underlying prejudice, namely, that things or objects given to us in experience, appear to us as continuously present. This is ultimately what is picked out by that unusual phrase bandied about by Heideggerians and Derrideans: the 'metaphysics of presence'. What is suppressed is the role that *absence* or *nothingness* plays in our experience and how most of our experience involves a constant interplay of presence and absence. Nothing, no object, is ever fully there and available to us as completely present in every particularity and possibility; indeed, Heidegger believes that this is obvious even in our experience of ordinary, everyday objects such as the chalk. When I say 'I see a piece of chalk over there', I mean or intend *that* piece of chalk, and *part* of what I mean or intend are aspects and possibilities of the chalk that are not actually present, or there, or continuously there before me. Consider for a moment something in your immediate vicinity, perhaps a lamp in the corner, a picture on the wall, a car passing by the window outside or in the distance; now consider what you *actually* perceive. It is one particular side that you see of, perhaps, the lampshade; a good portion of the object may actually be obscured from view, and yet we don't say that we see a part of a conical surface attached to what appears to be a supporting stem. We say that we see a lamp. In other words, we imagine the rest of the lamp to exist, we fill out the profile of the lamp imaginatively and synthesise this with what we currently perceive such that our intentional experience is not of something partially obscured but a fully conceived thing. Similarly, with the picture on the wall, we imagine that it is three-dimensional, has depth, and that there is a wall and hanging nail supporting the picture and the frame. In terms of the passing car, we might well say that we have heard a passing car, but what was actually given to us in terms of bare perception? It may only have been a sound or a series of sounds that reached our ears, and yet what we 'heard' was not a series of bare auditory sensations. What we 'heard' was a car that was not slowing down to turn into a driveway, rather we heard the sound of a car travelling with sufficient speed so as to suggest that it was driving on by the house. We *hear*, in that case, something very different from what we hear when we hear our own spouse's car turning into the driveway, the unmistakeable sound of the way they let the car idle before turning in and the full, vibrating baritone of the heavy diesel engine of that particular vehicle. As Heidegger explains in 'The Origin of the Work of Art',

> We never really first perceive a throng of sensations, e.g., tones and noises, in the appearance of things — as this thing-concept alleges; rather we hear the storm whistling in the chimney, we hear the three-motored plane, we hear the Mercedes in immediate distinction from the Volkswagen. Much closer to us than all sensations are the things themselves. We hear the door shut in the house and never hear acoustical sensations or even mere sounds. In order to hear a bare sound we have to listen away from things, divert our ear from them, i.e., listen abstractly. (BW, 151–52)

Similarly with other objects which are 'experienced', what the perceiver may actually be presented with is often a rather partial, obscured view and yet their imagination spontaneously fills out the rest of the profile of the thing which they don't actually see — the back of the lampshade which is absent is somehow made present by the imagination without actually being directly perceived during that experience. This insight fits nicely with Heidegger's belief that we artificially render everything as fully present to ourselves without realising that some of the aspects and features which we make 'present' are not currently present in our experience; rather, we project them onto our experience. This way of experiencing absence in presence and presence in absence is inherent to the structure of meaning and what 'is'. But it is when we forget or suppress this absence-presence, focusing entirely on the present, that we are left with a skewed metaphysical picture whereby the temporal, historical character of existence is concealed from us.

As we discussed previously, Heidegger had been vigorously pursuing some of these ideas through his teachings, writings and research all through the 1920s. Heidegger's ideas were already beginning to take shape, as evidenced by the extraordinary impact that he had on a generation of Germany's finest young philosophical minds who came to hear his lectures. This is made all the more extraordinary by the fact that Heidegger was a virtual nobody, quite young by academic philosophy's standards and with no major publications to speak of. And yet, by the time Heidegger was coming to the end of his years in Marburg and before the publication of *Being and Time*, he had acquired a cult status among young intellectuals in Germany. Clearly, the philosophical bombshell that was *Being and Time* had not happened overnight but had been about a decade in the making.

Heidegger's long labours into diverse parts of the history of philosophy began to take concrete shape around a number of core ideas. He was firstly greatly impressed by what he took to be the proto phenomenology of Aristotle. He was also convinced that a new brand of phenomenology, unencumbered with the transcendental baggage of the later Husserl, was the appropriate method, while recognising that time (or temporality) should be central to any attempt to begin to investigate the meaning of being. Heidegger had also absorbed some ideas from his theological studies, in particular the hermeneutical method, and decided that the manner in which he would pursue a phenomenological investigation into the meaning of being was through a hermeneutics of facticity—that is, an interpretation of our ordinary everyday existence. Rather than beginning with some abstract theory or idea, Heidegger insisted that we should begin with ordinary, everyday existence, before any abstractions. We look, that is, at our pre-reflective understanding and consider whether we can garner any clues as to why things are interpreted by us in the ways that they are, before we begin abstracting from the ordinary experience of what is closest to us.

The first division of *Being and Time* contains the famous 'existential analytic'[7] where Heidegger examines the sort of everyday environment that Dasein finds itself in. Contrary to what has often been suggested by advocates of the 'discontinuity thesis',[8] this does not reflect a tendency towards anthropocentrism on Heidegger's part, nor is this a consequence of his excessive prioritising of human subjectivity in his earlier work. Heidegger's goal is to answer the question concerning the meaning of being in general, and he offers a number of reasons for beginning with Dasein as part of that undertaking. Dasein[9] is such that its being is already a matter of significance for it—that is, it already has a sense of what it means by the word 'being' before we begin to analyse anything. In other words, and this is what the phrase 'hermeneutic circle' refers to, Heidegger begins with Dasein since it already has some kind of rough understanding of being which can be interrogated in terms of the way we are and things are for us in our everyday environment. On the basis of the way things already 'are', Heidegger believes we can begin to see what sorts of meaning the word being already has for us. Through an interpretation of our everyday world that excavates and sifts through the structures of our everyday experience, looking for the various ways in which things matter or mean something to us before we begin to abstract or theorise about them, Heidegger hopes to uncover some clues as to what being means for Dasein at some kind of primordial level. This is consistent with Heidegger's lifelong efforts *not* to make the meaning of being something that Dasein determines but something which is part of how Dasein understands itself before any abstraction. Dasein is therefore in an interpretive circle: we already have an understanding of being which is operative in our everyday world. Heidegger proposes to inquire after the meaning of being in general by asking after the meaning of being which is already at work, pre-reflectively, in the self-understanding of the human being. This is a circle which one cannot escape and should not try to escape. On the contrary, the circle is something that needs to be self-consciously embraced. Moreover, the meaning of being is not simply the consequence of Dasein imposing meaning on the world around it; rather, we find ourselves *thrown* into a world and an environment which is already revealing itself to us as meaningful before we even begin to interpret or examine the things around us.

Having said as much, the idea that things could be 'meaningful' independent of our experience of them is a somewhat baffling idea, for this reader at least. Granted, some Heidegger scholars have taken Heidegger's attempts to underline the fact that Dasein does *not* actively determine the meaning of being or that it is not dependent on Dasein's 'agency' in order to become meaningful to be proof that Heidegger is, among other things, a 'realist'. They further claim that in his later work, where he is trying more and more to undermine the attempts to read his early work as existentialism or anthropology or as a Dasein-oriented story, that we should understand him to be pursuing some kind of Heideggerian realism. Again, this is based on an interpretation of Heidegger's later texts in conjunction with an interpretation of *Being and Time* that I find unconvincing, along with what I take to be a misreading of Heidegger's own self-interpretations and criticisms of his earlier project. One obvious response to such approaches would be to say that the simple admission that an individual or group of individuals are not responsible for inventing the manner in which things can be meaningfully present is not to say that Heidegger thinks that things are revealing themselves as meaningful even if there is or are no individuals around for which anything can have meaning. That is not to say that he thinks that the planet or the objects within it no longer exist—the tree falling in the wood still falls, it still creates a disturbance, but it does not make the 'sound' that a person might 'hear' since hearing is intentional. This in part explains some of Heidegger's controversial comments and claims concerning animals in a number of places. For Heidegger, the animal is 'world poor' or 'poor in world' (*weltarm*). That does not mean that animals don't live, have feelings, experience things, but they do *not* share in a world where things become meaningful against a certain horizon in the ways that it does for Dasein. The same is true of rocks and plants; indeed, Heidegger will refer to stones as worldless (*weltlos*). He will go even further still in his 1935 lecture course, *Introduction to Metaphysics*, describing animals as worldless—'World is always *spiritual* world. The animal has no world *Welt*, nor any environment *Umwelt*' (IM, 47).

In the first division of *Being and Time* then, Heidegger, true to his word, examines in great detail the nature of the everyday world that we inhabit. He looks at the various elements of a compound structure which he refers to as being-in-the-world, since, for Heidegger, to 'be', for us, is to 'be in a world'. What Heidegger discovers in this protracted series of analyses is that we live, for the most part, in a project-oriented world, using various items and pieces of equipment at our disposal in order to secure some end or other. We are constantly in the process of trying to do or achieve something, we use x in order to do y; for example, perhaps you are currently using a Kindle or some such device in order to read this book; if you are reading the print edition, you may have a pen or pencil which you use to underline something you find interesting, or perhaps you have turned on a lamp so that the page is sufficiently illuminated, and so on. Our existence isn't entirely aimless; there is a direction to our activities. For instance, the reader of this book might be trying to learn about Heidegger before taking an introductory philosophy class at a university. The same person subsequently studies and tries to prepare for exams; if they do well in their exams they can progress to the next year and another two semesters of coursework, essays and exams. After their final exams, they will get a degree; they obtain a degree in the hope of making themselves an attractive proposition to potential employers. They go for interviews so that they can get a job—on and on this ceaseless striving for some goal or other goes until these goals all terminate one day in our non-existence. Within these various long-term projects, one is constantly doing various things in order to achieve or secure something else; one opens one's laptop to take notes for class, the lecturer uses a memory stick to store a PowerPoint presentation which she shows to the students—these various quotidian activities are always for the sake of some other goal such as the ones outlined earlier. Heidegger excavates and sifts his way through all of these aspects of our everyday being-in-the-world and begins to draw some conclusions: everything we do seems to be run through with a 'concern' of sorts. That is, we want to do various things and are 'concerned' with achieving things; moreover, there is a kind of urgency in what we do. Part of what Heidegger is already on the scent of here is the role that time plays for us.

So what is Heidegger trying to get at? Well, imagine a situation or task that you would really rather avoid—perhaps the prospect of asking someone out on a date. For other people, it might be something else that seems terribly daunting. Why on earth would we force ourselves to go through with something that we find so nerve-wracking or difficult? And why, on many occasions, do we force ourselves to do things sooner rather than later? The answer is quite simple: if we knew we were going to live forever, then we might not feel any urgency at all. The fact that we already know that our time is limited means that we are motivated to get things done. The world would appear very differently to us; what it *means to be*, what the being of things mean would be completely different if we were not finite creatures. This, in sum, is one of the fundamental insights of *Being and Time*, but Heidegger does not arrive at this insight cheaply—it is based on painstaking, thoroughgoing analysis of our everyday existence and the structures he discovers underlying it. Again, the point here is not to comment on the human condition or to contribute to existentialism. If we cast our minds back to the 1935 lecture course examined at the beginning of this chapter, we might begin to understand what Heidegger is up to. Remember, Heidegger is not interested in human beings per se; he is not trying to offer an anthropology or contribute to existentialism. Heidegger is interested in finding out what being means by looking at the way we already operate with an understanding of being in our day-to-day activities. Earlier we saw that Heidegger wanted to draw attention to the concealed backdrop to the way anything can be said to 'be' for us by rescuing or resuscitating the role of possibility in the way we experience anything or in which anything can be said 'to be'. His next move is to try to trace the way he might discover 'possibility' through this analysis of the everyday existence of Dasein. Now that he has uncovered the care or concern which he sees as the affective heart of our being-in-the-world, he wants to see how this is so. He will demonstrate that possibility, or more specifically, aspects of our own being which cannot be conflated with continuous presence, are part of what it means for us to be at the most fundamental level. Heidegger hopes to secure this as a result which will then justify the attempt to undertake a fundamental ontology, but all on the basis of a painstaking examination of the phenomena.

Having looked at our ordinary, everyday, pre-reflective being-in-the-world, Heidegger is able to determine that underlying everything we do is a concern with our existence—that is, things matter to us; we 'care'. We have a concern or care for our existence, the various projects we are involved in and the people with whom we share our world. Heidegger further suggests that we are always and ever in some kind of mood.[10] We find ourselves in a mood, we are never devoid of mood, and again, by sifting and excavating, Heidegger believes that we discover that the most basic mood of all is anxiety, or angst. This mood supersedes all others and sits as the backdrop to all our moods, to any mood that we find ourselves in at any given moment.

Again, if we examine anxiety with sufficient care, what we will eventually see is that behind all of our concerns and cares, we always have a sense of something outstanding, something that remains to be finished. There is a directionality to our lives, and at no point are we fully contained within a given moment. We are constantly being pulled forward to what comes next. What we see in a moment of authentic anxiety is that that which we are being pulled towards is the possibility which is the ultimate possibility that conditions and determines all of our more immediate or proximate possibilities. And that possibility, of course, is death—the possibility which we cannot escape and which outstrips all of our other possibilities.

A common misconception of Heidegger's discussion of death in *Being and Time* involves the belief that he is offering some kind of dark, morbid meditation on the human condition akin to various bleak existentialist accounts of human existence that began to proliferate in the middle part of the twentieth century and that were popularized by various writers. However, Heidegger is not interested in the actual event of death at all. Rather, Heidegger is interested in the idea that the manner in which we understand everything in the world around us is very heavily influenced and determined by the fact that our possibilities are not limitless but rather that we are temporally limited or finite creatures. In the same way that part of what it means for the chalk to be is to be its possibilities, possibilities that are not currently actual or there, so Dasein always *is* its possibilities, it *is* always 'towards' its future.[11] Incorporating this knowledge self-consciously into the way we live our lives can enrich it and make it a more authentic existence, according to Heidegger, as opposed to one where we live in something of an atemporal vacuum, taking everything for granted as though we will live forever. In this tranquillised, illusory everydayness we live a somewhat shallow existence where death, for example, is always something 'actual' (and thus something that has already happened to someone else) as opposed to our most immediate and basic 'possibility'. And, if Heidegger can secure possibility as part of what it means for anything to be for Dasein, including Dasein itself, then the notion of absence or nothingness can be restored to the metaphysical picture, because possibilities are precisely what are not yet present, and so Heidegger can set about overcoming the metaphysics of presence.

Consider the following scenario: suppose a professional athlete sets themselves the goal of winning a gold medal at the Olympics; they train and prepare and push themselves for years with this one singular goal in mind. They make their national team through qualifying competitions, then go to the Olympics and compete for their country. They qualify for the semi-finals and the final and, lo and behold, they win the gold medal. Right at that moment when they are presented with the gold medal, there is a simultaneous realisation that this moment is transient; they want to savour the moment, hold on to it but they know that they cannot. It is a momentary experience and part of what makes it so precious is that it passes, that it is fleeting. We cannot live in those moments indefinitely and that is part of what makes those moments so special. If they lasted forever, then they would *matter* to us in very different ways, or if, instead, we were to live on indefinitely, the *way* things matter to us as temporally unlimited creatures would be very different. The manner in which anything would 'be' for us would be different. Our finitude then is a crucial component in terms of the way things are meaningful to us. The way anything is for us—that is, the manner in which anything appears to us *as* something—is profoundly dependent on the fact that we experience the world as historical or temporally limited creatures. Any attempt at an ontology that fails to incorporate the implications of this insight is already operating within a problematic metaphysical framework according to Heidegger, and this is essentially his diagnosis of what has been going on in Western philosophy since Plato. Heidegger wants to move then from the metaphysics of presence to an ontology which realises the role that possibility, and thus absence or nothingness, play in terms of what it means for things to be. This is something that he thinks he can discover without abstracting from our ordinary everyday experience, and, on the basis of the clues he discovers there, Heidegger hopes to inaugurate or find a way back to a new or different way of thinking. He first plans to undertake this task in *Being and Time*— that is, he hopes to provide a fundamental ontology and conceives of the possibility of deconstructing the history of Western metaphysics and founding metaphysics anew. In time this aspiration evolves into the attempt to overcome metaphysics by finding a way back to a point preceding the first beginning of Western metaphysics to a new beginning where being would not reduce to presence. He explicitly relates this later project back to some of the key insights and aspirations of *Being and Time* but this is something which is sometimes ignored by proponents of the discontinuity thesis.

Being and Time is a very rich, densely argued text, and it is almost impossible to offer a general overview of such a nuanced, detailed and variegated philosophical work in a few pages. However, one of the things that simply cannot be emphasised enough is the role that 'possibility' plays in Heidegger's masterpiece. The failure to see this and the concomitant plans for a fundamental ontology that would finally free itself from the metaphysics of presence leads to all kinds of misinterpretations of the text. As we glossed previously, some Heidegger scholars take Heidegger to be overly wedded to a subjectivist and anthropological investigation in *Being and Time*, arguing that this was one of the fatal flaws of the book, leading him to abandon the project. However, other scholars, myself included, argue that this misunderstands what Heidegger is trying to do in *Being and Time*. Heidegger is not simply trying to offer an analysis of the human condition, nor is he trying to contribute to what was coming to be known on the Continent as existentialism. Heidegger does not even focus on the human being or human subjectivity in *Being and Time*. He begins with the notion of 'Dasein' and the kind of world it finds itself thrown into before one begins to abstract from or theorise about that world. He focuses on Dasein's ordinary being-in-the-world in the hope of finding clues as to how being is already understood in all manner of experiences before we begin to conceptualise things. What Heidegger ultimately finds is that, in the historical character of our everyday existence, we already see something like the role that possibility plays in the way things become meaningful for us, including ourselves and other people, such that we see the interplay of presence and absence in the way things present themselves as meaning anything at any given moment. From here, Heidegger hoped that he could begin to delineate the possibility of a new way of thinking, what he later characterises as an attempt at another or new beginning. This, ultimately, explains why Heidegger explicitly distances himself from any interpretations that involve straightforwardly partitioning his work into periods labelled as Heidegger I and Heidegger II, as he explained in the letter to Richardson, which the latter used as a preface for his famous book:

> One need only observe the simple fact that in *Being and Time* the problem is set up outside the sphere of subjectivism—that the entire anthropological problematic is kept at a distance, *that the normative issue is emphatically and solely the experience* of Therebeing [Dasein] with a constant eye to the Being-question—for it to become strikingly clear that the 'Being' into which *Being and Time* inquired can not long remain something that the human subject posits. It is rather Being, stamped as Presence by its timecharacter, that makes the approach to There-being [Dasein]. As a result, even in the initial steps of the Being-question thought is called upon to undergo a change whose movement *cor-responds* with the reversal. And yet, the basic question of *Being and Time* is not in any sense abandoned by reason of the reversal. Accordingly, the prefatory note to the seventh unrevised edition of *Being and Time* (1957) contains the remark: This 'way still remains even today a necessary one, if the question about Being is to stir our There-Being [Dasein]'. Contrary [to what is generally supposed], the question of *Being and Time* is decisively ful-filled in the thinking of the reversal. (Richardson, 2003, xviii)

Richardson himself seems to have agreed with the spirit of Heidegger's insistent claim here and underlines the continuity between the early Heidegger, who engaged in phenomenology, and the later Heidegger, who took up what he simply called 'thought'. However, other scholars keen to defend a discontinuity reading of Heidegger tend to perpetuate the notion of a sharp division between Heidegger I and II in ways that fly in the face of Heidegger's preface to Richardson's study and indeed many of Richardson's own carefully worked out conclusions. In one of many such retrospectives on his early project, Heidegger attempts to counter what he takes to be misreadings of his work that continue to abound to this very day:

> In *Being and Time* Dasein still stands in the shadow of the 'anthropological', the 'subjectivistic', etc.—and yet the opposite of all of this is what we have in view. . . . [In *Being and Time*] 'understanding of being' and *projecting-open* [are thought]—*and indeed as thrown*! The *being-in-the-world* of Dasein. But 'world' [is] not the Christian *saeculum* and the denial of god or atheism! World [is experienced] from within the essential sway of truth and of the t/here [*Da*]! World and earth (cf. lecture on the work of art). (CP, 208)

Daniel Dahlstrom summarises the issue with characteristic cogency and lucidity in his recent reference book on Heidegger:

> Heidegger planned a second part [of *Being and Time*], aimed at dismantling the history of ontology's myopic equation of being with presence. Yet he aborted the project because the metaphysical language he was employing distorted what he was endeavouring to say. Indeed, while he conceived SZ [*Sein und Zeit*] as an attempt to raise a transforming question that metaphysics traditionally failed to pose, he came to realise that his reliance upon the language of metaphysics led readers of SZ to a basic misunderstanding of it. Exemplifying this reliance is the talk of 'conditions of the possibility' and time as the 'transcendental [constantly present] horizon' of the understanding of being (SZ, 41). The tendency of contemporaries to take SZ's existential analysis to be a version of existentialism, a phenomenological existentialism with Dasein in the role of a transcendental subject, also betrays a fundamental misunderstanding of the text. (Dahlstrom, 2013, 3–4)

Heidegger returned to Freiburg in 1929 to take up the chair vacated by Edmund Husserl. Husserl had canvassed on Heidegger's behalf and played a large part in ensuring that Heidegger be taken on as his replacement. When he read *Being and Time*, Husserl was dismayed to find that Heidegger had no intention of furthering the cause of Husserl's project of transcendental phenomenology. Heidegger's return to Freiburg must have been something of a personal triumph. He held one of the most prestigious chairs in philosophy in Germany, was at the peak of his intellectual powers, and was now recognised as one of the most distinctive and important voices in philosophy as a result of the immediate impact of *Being and Time*. He had finally secured a much-coveted position in the university of his native region and the part of the world where he felt most at home. During this period of political upheaval, Heidegger's political sympathies went largely undetected, and he offered a number of lecture courses which testify to the extraordinary and evolving philosophical vision to which he remained committed.

NOTES

1. Raoul Mortley, 'Chapter I. Emmanuel Levinas' (1991). French Philosophers in Conversation, Paper 2. http://epublications.bond.edu.au/french_philosophers/2.

2. On the recommendation of Hartmann, who assured the faculty that Heidegger was on the verge of publishing an outstanding piece of work, Heidegger was put forward to replace Hartmann as a full professor. However, the ministry in Berlin rejected the proposal, insisting that Heidegger lacked the requisite level of internationally recognised publications commensurate with such a post. Later, samples of *Being and Time* were forwarded to the ministry, who stood by their original judgement. It was not until *Being and Time* was published as an offprint in the *The New Yearbook for Phenomenology* that the powers that be realised just what a philosophical force Heidegger was. Again, this supports the point we made against the claim that in the mid-1920s in Germany, Heidegger was widely recognised as a philosopher without equal.

3. In a famous 1932 paper, Carnap had tried to argue that logical analysis demonstrated that Heidegger's views in his 1929 lecture, 'What Is Metaphysics?', were literally nonsensical (see Carnap, 1932).

4. The kind of circularity involved is what Heidegger calls the hermeneutic circle which we will discuss shortly.

5. That is not to suggest that Heidegger's understanding of logic would have corresponded with what we would think of as the field of logic today. The notion of logic had a much broader scope in the early decades of the twentieth century than now. Notwithstanding, Heidegger's conception of logic, though different from ours, is still relevant to the concerns of the Vienna circle and the likes of Carnap. He explicitly refers to positivism in some of his writings in the 1930s and 1940s when returning to discuss his 1929 essay. Stephan Käufer makes a compelling case concerning the importance of the contextual backdrop to Heidegger's claims concerning logic as a graduate student and in his early years as a lecturer—that is, prior to the publication of *Being and Time*. Käufer argues, plausibly, that the notion of logic that loomed largest for Heidegger was a neo-Kantian one which was still quite distinct from the symbolic logic which was about to take centre stage in the late 1920s and 1930s. However, a number of points are worth bearing in mind here. Heidegger fastens on the law of con-

contradiction in his 1929 lecture in a manner that clearly pits itself against what were the stock views of the logical positivism which was beginning to emerge as a result of interpretations of Wittgenstein's *Tractatus* and the work of members of the Vienna Circle. Moreover, in subsequent lecture courses in the 1930s, where Heidegger returns to the question of the nothing, he responds to his positivist critics and directly refers to the 'positivism' of the day. Käufer is quite right that Heidegger is not sponsoring irrationalism, but to suppose that none of what he was arguing in 1929 was in any way relevant to the positivism that was emerging from the Vienna circle and which was already (rightly or wrongly) associated with Wittgenstein's 1912 *Tractatus* is unwarranted and doesn't really stand up to scrutiny (see Käufer, 2001).

6. Heidegger introduces here a dimension which seems to be implicit to *Being and Time* but which was not fully developed therein; he now acknowledges that Dasein itself is deeply implicated and affected by asking this question. It should come as no surprise then to see Heidegger begin to speak of the fate of Dasein as resting on our raising the question of being anew but in an appropriate way: 'What we know about how such questioning happens is all too little and too crude. In this questioning, we seem to belong completely to ourselves. Yet it is this questioning that pushes us into the open, provided that it itself, as questioning, transforms itself (as does every genuine questioning), and casts a new space over and through everything' (IM, 32).

7. The existential analytic involves, very much as the name suggests, an analysis of existence. And, of course, the kind of existence that Heidegger proposes to analyse is the ordinary, everyday existence of Dasein.

8. As discussed earlier in the context of Richardson's division of Heidegger's philosophy into Heidegger I and Heidegger II, numerous Heidegger scholars have been committed to a variety of interpretations which insist on a sharp *discontinuity* between *Being and Time* and the 'later' Heidegger.

9. As glossed earlier, Heidegger insists on referring to Dasein instead of 'person' or 'subject'. This is because Heidegger believes that these terms are already corrupted with the metaphysical baggage which he is trying to jettison. By Dasein, then, Heidegger is referring to the kind of existence that a human being has, but focusing on the existential, active character of that existence rather than treating it as an object which is there—simply and continuously present.

10. Heidegger is quick to distinguish his notion of *Befindlichkeit*, which is called a 'bare mood' or basic attunement in *Being and Time*, from feelings which are in fact a way of diverting us away from the 'nothing' which is what he is looking to investigate. Such feelings, psychic phenomena, directed or thematic moods, if you like, are taken up with things or matters in the world of everyday concern. Heidegger is looking for something else, however; he asks: 'Does such an attunement, in which man is brought before the nothing itself, occur in human existence? This can and does occur, although rarely enough and only for a moment, in the fundamental mood of anxiety. By this anxiety we do not mean the quite common anxiousness, ultimately reducible to fearfulness, which all too readily comes over us. Anxiety is basically different from fear. We become afraid in the face of this or that particular being that threatens us in this or that particular respect' (BW, 100). Heidegger has in mind a kind of anxiety that is not specifically directed then. He is thinking of a 'fundamental mood', something which is there, simmering away behind all our directed experience and which reaches up fully into our conscious awareness only rarely. But there is some sense of it whispering away in the background, just out of earshot, in a manner that we perhaps register as background noise that never leaves us entirely alone

in any particular moment of existence. When anxiety comes into full view for us, we are not anxious in a specific way, we are anxious before nothing in particular; all things that normally have significance are suddenly robbed of that same significance, they recede from our concern and we are left anxious about, nothing in particular, anxious over, if you like, nothing. Heidegger believes in fact that in the most basic occurrence of Dasein, the nothing is revealed; this is what anxiety discloses, but anxiety understood now as a fundamental mood, a bare mood, a basic attunement of our awareness, a fundamental dispositional state. And, the nature of our everyday evasion, our absorption with things, is itself phenomenological testament to the nothingness which is disclosed in our most basic disposition/disposedness. We are normally turned toward things, we are preoccupied in one way or another and turned away from the prior experience of the Nothing. Our 'turned-awayness' testifies in fact to the Nothing which we are held out into—the manner in which we are a transcendence in that we are already beyond beings as a whole. To be Dasein is, in a way, to be non-static, moving, thus there is this constant bare sense of 'more than now', 'more than this' constantly at work in our awareness.

11. This is also something which is revealed in 'bare moods' in our basic thrown nature—the 'da' of Dasein.

FIVE
The 1930s

Politics, Art and Poetry

LANGUAGE

Language begins to emerge as one of Heidegger's key concerns in the 1930s as he paves the way for his many and various forays into poetry and the unique role of language for the rest of his career. Many critics and commentators treat Heidegger's turn to language and poetry, in particular the poetry of Hölderlin in the 1930s and 1940s, as indicative of his general move away from the project of *Being and Time*. However, when one considers that Heidegger's concern is with the *meaning* of being (he could hardly have been more explicit about this in *Being and Time*), and given that he thinks that precisely what we lack is an understanding of this 'word', namely, 'being', it should hardly come as any surprise that he is going to investigate and excavate language to look for clues from our tradition as to what this word could or should mean. In the *Introduction to Metaphysics* he is quite explicit about the necessity of turning to language once one has clarified the depth and import of the problem concerning the question of being.[1]

Heidegger's fascinating voyages and explorations into language are somewhat tarnished by his indefensible chauvinism concerning any language apart from German, with the exception of ancient Greek.[2] This chauvinism itself is bound up with some of his more insalubrious political views. An unfortunate consequence of such prejudice has been the jaundiced attitude it has engendered in some of his interpreters towards other languages. Petzet, though not exactly an important philosophical voice, offers a typical enough example of this view. He is frequently guilty of arbitrary and ill-founded views concerning other languages, particularly English:

> A dangerous obstacle to communication is English, which is basically an unphilosophical language. Yet it is through English that Europeans gained philosophical access to the philosophical resources of the East. However rich English is in terms of vocabulary, it suffers a significant lack when it comes to *thinking*. (Petzet, 1993, 167)

And yet, Petzet never actually explains *why* English is so philosophically destitute, leading one to suppose that, like other notable disciples, he has simply unquestioningly inherited this prejudice from the Master. Heidegger did not read English and was certainly not proficient in the work of some of the great English-speaking philosophers. In describing Heidegger's interesting exchange with a Chinese monk at his home in Freiburg, Petzet notes again the difficulties they had with the English language. However, since the Monk speaks English and Petzet is translating for Heidegger, one might rather have supposed that their difficulties were more a consequence of their limited capacity with the English language than anything else. However, Petzet simply apes the Master again:

> Even what he [the monk] knows about Heidegger, he knows, besides through many oral communications, through English publications. Heidegger, looking concerned, doubts whether the crucial issues could be transmitted at all in that way, since the English language is completely unphilosophical. . . . English is much less philosophical than, for instance, French, in which a new word had to be constructed for what Heidegger means by *Sein* (being). (Petzet, 1993, 174)

Heidegger himself makes a relevant, if highly controversial, remark in his interview with *Der Spiegel*, where he claims that his French colleagues confirm repeatedly that the French language is simply not up to the task of philosophical thinking, which is why they revert to German the moment they wish to philosophise. Leaving to one side the appalling ethnic chauvinism which animates Heidegger's views on the primacy and superiority of the German language, we can see something of the effect that Heidegger exercises on those he came into contact with here. So many of Heidegger's philosophical acquaintances and intellectual friends simply inherited and perpetuated his views in an unquestioning manner. Petzet, in his laudatory remarks concerning Jean Beaufret, sheds light on Heidegger's bizarre aside in his interview with *Der Spiegel*:

> Whenever he [Beaufret] philosophised, he willingly switched to German, because he was of the opinion that things can be expressed better and more precisely in German than in French. (Petzet, 1993, 129)

Thus, we can see that Heidegger's reference to the 'French' in the context of his interview with *Der Spiegel* is in fact a direct reference to one of his most devoted acolytes—Jean Beaufret, who, while philosophically trained and an accomplished philosopher in his own right, was almost as uncritical with respect to Heidegger's thought as Petzet himself. Heidegger's exchange with his interviewers in the 1966 interview is worth reading.

> H: I have in mind especially the inner relationship of the German language with the language of the Greeks and with their thought. This has been confirmed for me today again by the French. When they begin to think, they speak German, being sure that they could not make it with their own language.
>
> S: Are you trying to tell us that that is why you have had such strong influence on the Romance countries, in particular French?
>
> H: Because they can no longer get by in the contemporary world with all their great rationality when it comes right down to understanding the world in the origin of its being. One can translate thinking no more satisfactorily than one can translate poetry. At best one can circumscribe it. As soon as one makes a literal translation everything is changed.

(Wolin, 1993, 113)

Despite the repellent nature of some of Heidegger's views in this regard, it would be a mistake to reject the entire undertaking outright as a result of these shortcomings; there are still some very important insights and observations which testify again to the creativity and originality of Heidegger's thinking. Heidegger's major objection to the romance languages is the crucial role played by their Latin foundations. Heidegger devotes considerable time and energy to demonstrating that something significant happens in the translation of ancient Greek ideas and terms into their Latin cognates. Heidegger further sees these shifts and changes as having decisive consequences for the history of the unfolding of Western philosophy. For Heidegger, there is significant distortion in the translation of these Greek terms into what are taken then as their Latin equivalents. One of Heidegger's most notorious examples concerns the ancient Greek word for truth: *aletheia*. The word is subsequently translated into Latin as *'veritas'*, which Heidegger believes to be deeply misleading in that it covers over or obscures the rich connotations of the Greek term and, in turn, forces Western thinking in a particular direction in terms of the very notion of truth. The Greek *aletheia* is a much richer word, Heidegger argues, than *veritas*. The Greek word is a combination of the alpha privative ('a') with the Greek word for oblivion or concealment, *lethe*. For Heidegger, the notion of truth has been narrowed through the initial choice of *veritas*, which, when it is absorbed into the Romance languages determines the range of meaning of 'truth'; that is, it constricts our understanding of the term 'truth' excessively. The notion of *veritas* confines itself to something like correctness and certainty, the correct correspondence of the object with the judgement concerning the object, or what is often referred to in philosophy as the correspondence theory of truth. For Heidegger, what the ancient Greek word for truth conveys beyond the notion of mere correctness then, is the notion of the 'un'-concealing or 'dis'-closure of something. This is the function of the alpha privative, and if the problem for Western thinking and culture has been a problem of the forgetting of or oblivion of the meaning of being (*Seinsvergessenheit*—literally 'forgetting of Being'), then it is fitting that the attempt at a recovering of what has been forgotten involves a reconception of truth, which involves the recovery of something from a state of oblivion or having been forgotten. Is it any wonder then that Heidegger's concern for the rest of his career revolves around what he calls the 'truth' of being—that is, the retrieval of something whose meaning has fallen into oblivion?

It is not possible here to do justice to the breadth and sophistication of Heidegger's examination of language, and there is a vast literature on the topic. However, one issue which must be confronted, now that we have had to re-evaluate Heidegger's philosophy since the publication of some of his lecture courses and seminars from the 1930s along with the *Black Notebooks*, is the antisemitism that seems to be operative in terms of Heidegger's views on the German language. This is something that I believe we need to reconsider in terms of Heidegger's confrontation with modernity more generally.³ Questions remain concerning the historical and cultural backdrop that seems to inform aspects of Heidegger's confrontation with modernity previously thought to be unproblematic. It might well be the case that the proposed theoretical relationship between Heidegger's philosophy and his antisemitism is adventitious, opportunistic and unessential in terms of the nuts and bolts of his thinking. However, we are also forced to confront the uncomfortable fact that other aspects of Heidegger's much lauded confrontation with modernity and his sweeping diagnosis of the history of Western metaphysics as a history of the metaphysics of presence are a variant on what were ultimately a series of stock antisemitic prejudices that proliferated in Germany from the late 1700s onwards.

A number of Heidegger's proposed measures in terms of countering what he refers to a number of times as the 'Jewification' of the modern era may well be only superficially related to some otherwise remarkable philosophical analyses which, themselves, do not necessitate any kind of racism. That does not take away from the fact that he is trying to find a way to justify his own political views and antisemitic sentiments, which themselves seem, to me at least, to belong to a tradition prejudiced against the Jews. Heidegger makes a number of pointed remarks concerning Judaism in the *Black Notebooks* and in his correspondence. He insists that it is world Jewry in particular that shapes the fundamental impulses of the calculative age, the technological age. Consider then Harry Redner's observation in a paper titled "Philosophers and Antisemitism":

> The Jew thus served as a scapegoat, a generalised symbol of exclusion.... The Jew was not only opposed to the German but, even more so, to the Greek, with whom the German was held to have a special kinship. The concept of the Aryan was formulated to express and account for this affinity on both linguistic and supposedly racial grounds, and this, too, served to exclude Jews who were presumed to exemplify the opposite racial type. Much of Western history was presented as an ongoing struggle between the Aryan and the Semite; and in this symbolic way many current issues were couched and supposedly explained. The neoclassical revival of Greek antiquity in Germany from Winckelmann onwards also frequently led in the same anti-Jewish and, at the same time, anti-Christian direction. Jewish Spirit was held to be infinitely inferior to Attic Spirit and unless it was rigidly excluded it would only taint and corrupt the rebirth of the classically noble and sublime in Germany. Nineteenth-century German

culture and scholarship was pervaded by these ideas. . . . In the twentieth century all this came to full fruition in the various kinds of antisemitic ideologies. (Redner, 2002, 116)

So, we have to ask ourselves whether in fact some of what Heidegger has to say belongs to a context that has not always been acknowledged or recognised. Heidegger's views on the inner affinity between the Greek and German languages are often glossed over since Heidegger's account of the translation of ancient Greek philosophical terms into Latin and the implications for the history of Western philosophy can be fascinating.[4] Yes, there is the odd arch of an eyebrow at the remarks he makes about the philosophical destitution of the French language in his 1966 interview that we quoted earlier; but all too often it is something that is simply accepted unquestioningly by Heideggerians. However, a question that we have to ask ourselves is whether these views, in the end, follow a recurring and worrisome pattern in Heidegger. This particular prejudice concerning the inner affinity between Germany and ancient Greece was longstanding. The basic gist of some of Heidegger's claims in this regard can be found in Fichte's[5] *Addresses to the German Nation*. In GA 95, Heidegger makes a number of pointed remarks on language:

> *Language.*—The Germans will not grasp—let alone fulfil—their Western destiny, unless they are equipped for it by the originality of their language, which must ever again find its way back to the simple, uncoined word, where the closeness of being bears and refreshes the imprintability of discourse. But at first the German language will be sacrificed to Latin-Italian phrasemongering, to journalistic flattening, and to 'technical' 'standardising'. (*Ponderings VII–XI*, 81)

Heidegger seems to launch a broadside against everything in the Western tradition that has led to modernity and eventually the age of technology. To be fair, he seems to lump Judaism into the melting pot along with everything else that he sees as a consequence of the history of the metaphysics of presence, a metaphysics which he believes the German people alone can overcome. However, how much of this is really just part of the antisemitic and nationalist sentiment which had been simmering away (and, of course, occasionally boiled over) in the nineteenth and early twentieth centuries? That is not to say that some of Heidegger's insights are not remarkable or that he is not a thinker of the first rank. But, for too long, it seems, we have not sufficiently excavated and identified what might well be the sinister (and at times disappointingly derivative) motivations behind what many took to be the unique features of Heidegger's confrontation with modernity, a confrontation which appears to share some of the same basic prejudices as a rampant antisemitism which had loomed large in German intellectual life since the beginning of the nineteenth century at the very least. Fichte, as we know, had some rather distressing things to say on the topic of the Jews in some of his earlier writings (1793):

> In the bosom of almost all the nations of Europe there spreads a powerful state driven by hostile feelings that is continually at war with all the others, and that in certain states terribly oppresses the citizens. I speak of Jewry [*Judentum*].
>
> As to giving them civil rights, I see no way other than that of some night cutting off their heads and attaching in their place others in which there is not a single Jewish idea. To protect ourselves from them I see no means other than to conquer for them their promised land and to pack them off there. (Fichte, 1973, 114ff.)[6]

To be fair, Fichte appears to have thought better of such remarks soon afterwards, and to the best of my knowledge, there are no further explicit remarks of this nature. It is also more than likely that the second remark was not meant to be taken literally (though it still stops one in one's tracks).[7] In what one commentator sees as an intensification of the revolutionary and antijudaic sentiment of Fichte, he concludes,

> The Jewish Question, in fact, was central to the revolutionism of the Wartburg. The seminar papers and diaries of German students of these angry years reveal a startling intensification of revolutionary hostility into an intellectual and emotional hatred of Judaism that demanded its total extirpation from German life. In the mouthings of these revolutionary students of 1812–1819 there are shocking glimpses of the real ancestry of Nazi antisemitism, including even the 'stab in the back' theme. (Rose, 1992, 126)

The same commentator also includes some outbursts from the likes of E. M. Arndt:

> One must prohibit and prevent the importation into Germany of Jews from abroad. . . . The Jews as Jews do not fit into this world and this state, and therefore I do not want their number to be unduly increased in Germany. I also do not wish this because

they are an alien race and because I desire to keep the Germanic race as pure as possible.

Consider Heidegger's complaints (in an admittedly less than guarded moment) in a 1916 letter to his wife:

> The jewification of our culture & universities is certainly horrifying & I think the German race really should summon up the inner strength to find its feet again. (LW, 28)

Then there are remarks such as the following from his notorious 1933–1934 Winter Semester seminar—*Nature, History, State*:

> For a Slavic people, the nature of our German space would definitely be revealed differently from the way it is revealed to us; to Semitic nomads, it will perhaps never be revealed at all. This way of being embedded in a people, situated in a people, this original participation in the knowledge of the people, cannot be taught, at most it can be awakened from its slumber. (NHS, 56)

Thus, we have to at least *consider* the possibility that such remarks belong, in some way, to a certain context or tradition.

It would be a terrible oversimplification to simply reduce Heidegger's philosophy to this kind of extreme nationalism and antisemitism (mind you, that does not stop many commentators from doing as much). Notwithstanding, it is worth pointing out that there had been a sustained attempt to put German revolutionary-nationalist sentiment on more of a spiritual, philosophically informed footing.[8] Fichte is portrayed by some commentators as something of an unwitting proto-spokesman for how these ideas began to take what appears to be a philosophical form. And, it seems to me at least, that some of Heidegger's bizarre attempts to relate his philosophical views to a renewal of German spiritual and cultural life under National Socialism belong, whether by accident or design, to something like this tradition.

The general pattern, then, is as follows: Heidegger held extreme nationalistic and antisemitic views, which appear to be in keeping with a certain tradition. He also had very little genuine political understanding or ability, but he did believe for a time that he had the capacity to act as spiritual leader for the National Socialist 'movement'. He thought that by serving in this way, he could realise his own version of the goals of a great, renewed German nation which would be at the vanguard of a renewal of the West and that would counter the ruthless frenzy of the 'gigantic' and 'calculative' spirit which he associates with world Jewry in particular.

Thus, despite what is taken at times to be an early critical attitude to National Socialism in the *Black Notebooks*, it is not that Heidegger was against antisemitism, the renewal of the German nation and spirit, all under the banner of National Socialism. Rather, Heidegger threw his own hat into the ring of contending voices, jockeying for influence and favour as potential spokespeople for the 'movement':

> Eucken made his feelings known to the pro-rector Sauer, who noted the incident in his diary: 'He said that Heidegger was acting as though he wanted to run the whole show himself, on the principle of the *Führer* system. He obviously saw himself as the natural philosopher and intellectual leader of the movement — and as the only great thinker since Heraclitus'. (Ott, 1993, 169)

Heidegger was convinced that the 'revolution' should be based on key elements of his own philosophical vision, namely, the attempt to overcome the metaphysics of presence and the inauguration of a new beginning which would stand as the unique opportunity and destiny of the German people in particular. Blood, stock and race, while important to an extent, are not the key notions for him in the revitalisation of the German people and the salvation of the West: the war is one that must ultimately be waged at the level of metaphysics. In this, one simply has to conclude that Heidegger was as naïve as he was megalomaniacal. Moreover, he demonstrates in his notebooks and elsewhere his willingness to make disparaging comments concerning the Jews and their influence — but again — this influence is felt ultimately and therefore must be confronted at the level of metaphysics since they are responsible for a large part of what characterises the gigantic and rootless nature of the modern technological age. There seems to be a serious question then as to just how much of Heidegger's thinking concerning the inner affinity of German and Greek experience and language is parasitic on a distinctly nationalistic and frequently antisemitic agenda that was simmering away in Germany from the early nineteenth century onwards. In terms of the blind and obstinate faith in the inner kinship between the Germans and the ancient Greeks, we see just how dogmatic Heidegger is on this issue. He wonders,

> whether **we**, whether precisely the Germans, are strong enough to assume this highest and most hidden care, the care for the truth of being.
>
> For **we** '*are*' kindred to the Greeks not in that we take them as models and guard them, perhaps especially and otherwise than

did mere 'humanism' and 'classicism'—but rather in that **we**, like the Greeks, have to venture the first beginning of Western history and carry out the completely *other* beginning. (*Ponderings VII–XI*, 145; emphasis added)

Furthermore, his supposed general attack on modernity seems to belong at times to a context which at the very least should give us pause:

> The 'victor' in this 'struggle,' which contests goallessness pure and simple and which can therefore only be a caricature of a 'struggle,' is perhaps the greater groundlessness that, not being bound to anything, avails itself of everything (Judaism). Nevertheless, the genuine victory, the one of history over what is a-historical, is achieved only where what is groundless excludes itself because it does not venture being but always only reckons with beings and posits their calculations as what is real. . . . One of the most concealed forms of the *gigantic*, and perhaps the oldest, is a tenacious facility in calculating, manipulating, and interfering; through this facility the worldlessness of Judaism receives its ground. (*Ponderings VII–XI*, 75–76)

> But the occasional increase in the power of Judaism is grounded in the fact that Western metaphysics, especially in its modern evolution, offered the point of attachment for the expansion of an otherwise empty rationality and calculative capacity, and these thereby created for themselves an abode in the 'spirit' without ever being able, on their own, to grasp the concealed decisive domains. (*Ponderings XII–XV*, 37)

Of course, in many of these passages, Heidegger is not just thinking about the primacy of the German language but is invoking a series of ideas that he clearly wants to link to his broadside against Modernity. Other themes that Heidegger begins to meditate on in the 1930s are poetry and art. What is undeniable now, and as we have seen in the foregoing, is just how politically oriented some of Heidegger's views were as he was developing these ideas.

ART AND POETRY

Before the 1930s, Heidegger had precious little to say on the subjects of art or poetry. Nevertheless, Heidegger had long been interested in the poetry of Hölderlin and, finally, in the early 1930s, this protracted engagement with Hölderlin's work begins to come to the fore. In 1934, Heidegger delivers the first of his Hölderlin lectures and the famous German poet remains a key influence for Heidegger's thinking for the rest of his career. An often overlooked feature of Heidegger's engagement with Hölderlin is the politically charged nature of that engagement. As one reads through the first lectures Heidegger delivers on Hölderlin, one cannot mistake the manner in which he situates his readings of Hölderlin within his larger political vision.

In 1935–1936, Heidegger drafted the text of his hugely influential essay (published in 1950), 'The Origin of the Work of Art', which was based on a series of lectures he gave in the mid-1930s. The essay has taken on something of a life of its own and is considered a 'classic' in terms of Continental approaches to aesthetics and the philosophy of art. Heidegger himself, however, was keen to distance his discussion of the notion of the origin of the artwork from any conventional theories of art or aesthetics. Again, what has often been overlooked is the overtly political nature of Heidegger's essay on the origin of the work of art. Heidegger is *again* calling on the unique destiny of the German people; Hölderlin is discussed as the poet the Germans need to listen to in order to foster the conditions necessary for an authentic 'happening' for the German people, a new political and cultural beginning, which represented the only possible salvation for the West, as Heidegger saw it.

Heidegger is interested in particular in how 'great' works of art allow us to see the way that a world gives shape to the meaningfulness of everything for us. Heidegger begins to describe this as the 'strife' between earth and world. Again, this can seem like an obscure set of ideas. Heidegger is tortuously inscrutable in his discussions of them, because he refuses to rely on 'ordinary' language, which he sees as inescapably mired in the metaphysics of presence. Discussions of Heidegger's meditation on the origin of the artwork can sometimes trade in a rather forbidding 'Heideggerese', a jargon that has developed around these ideas which has served to obfuscate and confuse more than it clarifies. That is not to lay too much blame at the door of Heidegger scholars; Heidegger's idiom is so unique and difficult at times that it is all too easy to fall into the habit of reproducing the jargon instead of unpacking it.

Through these interrelated notions of earth and world, Heidegger is trying to distinguish between something we might think of as the ground or the basis for anything which can manifest itself as a phenomenon for us (Heidegger is not thinking about the 'planet') and, on the other hand, the unique meaning-shaping function of a particular context, which he designates as a 'world'. This is what

Heidegger means when he discusses what can sound like a rather bizarre tongue twister: 'the world worlds' or the 'worlding of the world'. In other words, in terms of the unique way in which things emerge as meaningful for us, Heidegger thinks that he can outline the constitutive features of any and all such manifestations which themselves come under a more overarching story concerning the history of the unfolding of Western metaphysics as a metaphysics of presence or the history of the various epochal ways that things are revealed as meaningful for particular peoples.

Again, Heidegger develops some of these ideas in rather worrisome ways in the 1930s, and it is not at all clear that he ever fully abandons a version of the provincialism that he begins to weave into his philosophy through this period. He ends his essay on the origin of the work of art with an appeal or summons of sorts which, in the context of the political climate of the mid-1930s, leaves little enough to the imagination:

> Whenever art happens, whenever, that is, there is a beginning, a thrust enters history and history either begins or resumes. History, here, does not mean a sequence of events in time, no matter how important. History is the transporting of a people into its appointed task as the entry into its endowment. (OWA, 49)

What we eventually see in the closing lines of the essay is that Heidegger's initial engagement with Hölderlin is very much connected to his political views in the 1930s; Heidegger's later thought returns again and again to these themes and ideas, often in registers which are unmistakably similar. Heidegger's ultimate interest, then, is not really art, in this essay at least, nor is it conceived as a contribution to aesthetics. Heidegger is really only interested in establishing the manner in which a work of art allows us to see the way that a world shapes meaning or significance in very particular ways for a particular people. And, once he has established again that the central issue is the question of truth—that is, the way things are unconcealed in specific, historical ways, then he is able to move to a more specific discussion of Hölderlin and poetry, but all the while with his eye firmly fixed on a political philosophy which is more and less explicit depending on the context. He concludes the essay thus:

> Are we, in our existence, historically at the origin? Or do we, rather, in our relationship with art, appeal, merely, to a culture's knowledge of the past?

> For this either-or and its decision there is a certain sign. Hölderlin, the poet whose work stands before the Germans as a test, put it into words when he said
> Reluctant to leave the place
> Is that which dwells near the origin. (OWA, 50)

Again, as I mentioned previously, a disappointing trend, in terms of the way some of the literature deals with issues concerning the terminology and ideas Heidegger develops in his discussion of the role of poetry and art for a community, is the tendency to simply reproduce Heidegger's idiosyncratic language and neologisms. Heidegger's discussion concerning the strife between Earth and World can seem rather forbiddingly abstruse. However, the ideas themselves are not nearly so complicated as they might seem. There is a tendency at times to repackage Heidegger's philosophy such that it can begin to sound like some kind of mysticism, which has helped to consolidate the rather misleading caricature of Heidegger that obtains for philosophers less familiar with his work or who traditionally work in what is often referred to as the analytic or Anglo-American tradition. Certainly, the fact that Heidegger is struggling to articulate something which he believes has been overlooked by the tradition and in a language which is not already infected with the metaphysics of presence can lead to some rather unwieldy prose at times; nevertheless, it is worth bearing in mind that Heidegger is not trying to be obscure for the sake of obscurity. There is an anecdote that seems apposite in this context. Once, when Gadamer visited Heidegger in his hut in Todtnauberg, Heidegger began to read for his guest from an essay on Nietzsche that he was writing. Apparently, while reading aloud, Heidegger became exasperated and pounded his fist on the table declaring, 'This is all Chinese' (Gadamer, 2016, 244).

NOTES

1. The title of the second chapter of *Introduction to Metaphysics* is 'On the Grammar and Etymology of the Word "Being"'.
2. Heidegger insists that there is a special affinity between ancient Greek and the German language which does not obtain between ancient Greek and the Romance languages. Some of his keenest English-speaking interpreters tend to disparage non-German languages, in particular English, as hopelessly impoverished when it comes to discussing anything philosophically important. This blind obeisance to some of Heidegger's more egregious philosophical prejudices leads to some rather farcical linguistic gymnastics in terms of translating and interpreting Heidegger's work. A point that often seems lost on those who

place too much emphasis on this aspect of Heidegger's Germanophilia is the fact that this very prejudice is not exclusive to Heidegger, nor is he the first German philosopher to make this connection between the German language and ancient Greek. In his *Addresses to the German Nation*, for example, Fichte goes to some lengths to demonstrate an inner affinity between the Ancient Greek and German languages.

3. One of the more recent and certainly one of the most thought-provoking treatments of these issues was provided by Peter Trawny (2015).

4. Tom Rockmore takes up these questions in his essay in *Heidegger's Black Notebooks: Responses to Antisemitism*. Rockmore succumbs ultimately to an alarmist and philosophically unjustified conclusion, however, in that he wants to argue that 'Heidegger's philosophical theories are not unrelated to but rather linked to, even dependent on, his antisemitism'. However there is simply no real evidence to suggest that the rudiments of Heidegger's evolving and continuous philosophical vision are ultimately motivated by stock German antisemitism. And this seems to be simply the precipitous kind of leap one associates with the sensationalism and philosophically illegitimate strategies of Faye, with whom Rockmore clearly aligns himself. However, we do agree on one thing: Heidegger's attempts to marry his own history of Being with his political views borrow heavily from some longstanding antisemitic tropes from the German intellectual establishment and, furthermore, *some* of what are considered to be parts of Heidegger's innovative vision concerning the history of Western metaphysics reduce in the end to simple old-fashioned German nationalist antisemitism dressed up in Heideggerian jargon. However, the further step of reducing everything in Heidegger's philosophy to these unsavoury sources is simply unfounded and excessive. Rockmore sums up some of the more measured parts of his analyses nicely in the following paragraphs, where he discusses how Trawny believes that Heidegger's position 'became tinged with antisemitism. Each of these examples manifests a familiar kind of philosophical nationalism linked with antisemitism, namely the defense of the Germans, or at least what I will be calling 'real' or again 'true' Germans, combined with the view that Jews are not and cannot be Germans in a more than peripheral sense. The main theme seems to be as follows: a German must have roots that by definition a Jew cannot have, hence he (or she) cannot be German. This view was widely held during this period. Thus Bruno Bauch, the president of the Kant-Gesellschaft until 1916, notoriously held the opinion, which he published in *Kant-Studien* (1916), that a Jew simply could not become a German no matter how long he lived in Germany. German philosophical antisemitism early in the twentieth century continues a tradition in which Fichte played a prominent role. In the *Addresses to the German Nation*, more than a century before Heidegger, Fichte distinguished between Germans, in his view those who speak German, and all others. Fichte, who does not seem to have any background in linguistics, thinks German is the only modern language that preserves the insights of the ancient Greek and ancient Greece. Fichte's restrictive view, which once again distinguishes between authentic Germans and everyone else, was influential well into the twentieth century. "According to Hans Sluga, Heidegger modelled his *Rektoratsrede* on Fichte's text' (Rockmore, 2017, 162).

5. Johann Gottlieb Fichte (1762–1814) was a German philosopher often credited with inaugurating the philosophical movement known as German idealism. He is considered an important philosophical figure in his own right but is also sometimes seen historically as a bridging figure between Kant and Hegel.

6. Robert Bernasconi also makes a brief reference to this remark by Fichte in an illuminating essay in the recently published volume *Heidegger's Black Notebooks: Responses to Antisemitism* (see Bernasconi, 2017, 172–73).

7. As Bernasconi (2017) observes, 'It is quite staggering that anyone could employ that image in the context of a discussion of the French Revolution, written one year after the introduction of Joseph-Ignace Guillotin's guillotine' (173).

8. Sluga (1993) elaborates on this point with characteristic concision: 'The crisis so announced became historically activated by the outbreak of revolutions in America and France and eventually in Germany. There it was manifested in different form, however, since historical circumstances did not encourage real political and social revolutions. Germany produced substitutes. Thinkers first turned their attention to the revolutionary events in France, hoping or fearing that these might spill over into Germany, and then they forged the entirely new idea of a spiritual crisis. In this transformation the German philosophers of the period were essential, for they convinced themselves that, in step with the French revolution, there had taken place in Germany an even more important event—not an event in political life but one in the hidden depths of philosophy. . . . The political turnabout abroad could thus be seen to have its complement and completion in a philosophical revolution in Germany' (69).

SIX

The Nazi Rector

We have briefly glossed the political backdrop to some of Heidegger's work in the 1930s—it remains for us now to consider further some of the most controversial aspects of the Heidegger 'Affair'. In April 1933 Heidegger stunned many of even his closest friends, colleagues and students when he agreed to become the first Nazi rector of Freiburg University (he joined the Nazi party around the same time). For many of Heidegger's friends and colleagues, not to mention his Jewish students, this was a completely unanticipated turn of events, since, as far as they were concerned, there had been nothing in his demeanour or attitude to that point to suggest that he might be sympathetic to Nazism. In more recent years there has been some evidence of early sympathy for political and cultural currents which were important precursors to National Socialism, and it seems unlikely that Heidegger happened upon his political allegiances overnight in 1933. Nevertheless, in the main, Heidegger kept his political views close to his chest. There have been some reports of Heidegger having read and been impressed with elements of *Mein Kampf*,[1] and there is no denying his sympathy for antimodern views, provincialism and a conservative revolutionary outlook, all of which had been percolating within Germany. What is most surprising, perhaps, is the growing evidence of Heidegger's undeniable antisemitism. Granted, it would be unfair to portray Heidegger as another Julius Streicher;[2] however, one cannot but be dismayed that a man who had had a passionate love affair with Hannah Arendt, who clearly respected the early phenomenology of

Edmund Husserl and nurtured the philosophical development of numerous Jewish students, would, nonetheless, harbour and indeed openly express the antisemitic sentiments which we find in his notebooks, correspondence and seminars.

There has been a recurring controversy surrounding the relationship between Heidegger's philosophy and his political views, actions, writings and speeches during the 1930s, which has proved one of the most ill-tempered intellectual affairs of the twentieth and (now twenty-first) century. The initial fallout was a sense of complete betrayal on the part of Heidegger's Jewish students and colleagues.[3] Though Husserl had converted to Catholicism as a young man, he was, nonetheless, a Jew and was deeply affronted not just by Heidegger's actions in 1933 but also at what he perceived to be an increasing level of antisemitism in his one-time protégé.[4] Other notable students such as Herbert Marcuse, Karl Löwith, Hannah Arendt, Leo Strauss and Hans Jonas, among others, were shocked at Heidegger's behaviour, never having seen any evidence before then that Heidegger might have held such deeply offensive political views and ethnic prejudices.[5] Notwithstanding, after the war, Heidegger somehow managed to successfully peddle an 'official story' concerning his involvement with the Nazi party which had a lot of traction with Heideggerians until relatively recently.

The Heidegger controversy is a complicated and messy affair. However, it is an issue that should have and could have been dealt with comprehensively and exhaustively a long time ago. Several factors have contributed to the enduring nature of this controversy, which continues to flare up with a vengeance every other decade or so. On the one hand, the fact that some of Heidegger's most troublesome writings and texts have been drip-fed to the public over an agonizingly protracted period has had the effect of suggesting that even more dreadful Nazi spectres lurk among the unpublished texts. Another major problem lies in the fact that the preponderance of the commentators who *have* made significant studies on the question of Heidegger's involvement with National Socialism and the consequences for his thought are operating, frankly, with an inadequate facility with Heidegger's philosophy and thus are guilty of non-sequiturs, misinterpretations, rash conflations along with a whole series of other interpretive foibles.

In 1987, for example, the French intellectual scene was rocked by the publication of Victor Farias's book on the controversy. The book was also translated into English and a whole generation of interpreters of Heidegger's work were forced to sit up and take notice (see Farias, 1989). Farias's book contained a good deal of incriminating evidence (though it has to be said that most of this had already been brought to light by Hugo Ott in his political biography on Heidegger) but suffered from a conspicuous interpretive handicap: Farias was completely out of his depth in terms of trying to connect Heidegger's philosophy with his political views. As a consequence, many commentators, some of whom did eventually try to tackle the controversy themselves, were able to readily dismiss Farias's book as juvenile and ill-informed.[6] Richard Wolin imported the controversy into North America, hot on the heels of the controversy that erupted in France, and published a series of controversial shorter pieces by Heidegger from the 1930s. He included interviews and essays by students and colleagues of Heidegger concerning the controversy, as well as a translation of Heidegger's interview with *Der Spiegel*. The collection itself is somewhat tendentious in that there is a significant amount of editorial staging and packaging by Wolin, not least in terms of his brief introductions to the pieces he selects for publication and in terms of the lopsided nature of the commentaries and retrospectives he includes in the collection. Nevertheless, it remains a useful compendium if one can manage to circumvent these editorial improprieties. Wolin also published his own monograph on the controversy around this time, *The Politics of Being*. However, this book is guilty of some of the problems that hamstring Farias's text. Emmanuel Faye published by far and away the most problematic text on the Heidegger controversy in 2005; the book was translated into English with great fanfare in 2009. Faye goes way beyond any of his predecessors in terms of the accusations he levels against Heidegger. The subtitle of the book alone is enough to give pause: *The Introduction of Nazism into Philosophy*. Thomas Sheehan famously traded blows with Faye at a conference on the *Black Notebooks* in New York in 2014. Sheehan expanded his challenges to Faye into a controversial paper in which he argues that Faye is either a fraud or an incompetent when it comes to the subject of Heidegger's philosophy and its relevance to his political views in the 1930s (see Sheehan, 2015).

The most recent eruption of the controversy began when Peter Trawny drew attention to the imminent publication of three volumes of Heidegger's private notebooks from the 1930s and 1940s, which Trawny himself had edited. Owing in part, no doubt, to the extremely disturbing nature of the passages from the notebooks which Trawny drew attention to prior to their publication, the ensuing controversy proceeded in exactly the same manner as on previous occasions, and before the notebooks had even been published. Militant proponents of a particular brand of analytic philosophy, who have a rather dubious agenda in terms of the ideological stance they adopt concerning appropriate philosophical method, used these 'leaked' passages to jump on the anti-Heidegger bandwagon once more, making it all too easy for the Heideggerian faithful to fend off these trivial attacks and maintain fortress Heidegger. While the other critical voices were led by ideologically motivated commentators who knew as little about Heidegger's philosophy as the analytic commentators who dismissed Heidegger without reading him. This superficial controversy managed to conceal the deep underlying philosophical questions which *must* be put to Heidegger's thought. These are questions that bear on our reading of *Being and Time* and Heidegger's antimodernism more generally; after all, Heidegger genuinely believed that he could articulate a political philosophy based on what he took to be foundational elements of his philosophical outlook.

Related to this problem is the fact that Heidegger linked elements of his thought to appalling forms of ethnic chauvinism, including, but not confined to, antisemitism, as we have seen earlier. Notwithstanding, it would be terribly unfair to characterise Heidegger as a bloodthirsty biological racist, but Heidegger was very much an archconservative, German traditionalist and prone to some rather bizarre provincialist notions which he tried to justify philosophically. One can see Heidegger looking to explicitly incorporate these views into his philosophy in a radio address from 1934 'Why We Remain in the Provinces' and again in his influential 1959 text 'Memorial Address' where he introduces the term *Gelassenheit*.[7] Even as late as 1966, Heidegger reaffirms his belief that democracy is not the key to finding a way to live authentically in a technological world. In the aforementioned interview with *Der Spiegel*, Heidegger declares,

> Meanwhile in the past thirty years it should have become clearer that the global movement of modern technology is a force whose scope in determining history can scarcely be overestimated. A decisive question for me today is: how can a political system accommodate itself to the technological age, and which political system would this be? I have no answer to this question. I am not convinced that it is democracy. (Wolin, 1993, 104)

Considering the manner in which Heidegger had looked to marry his own provincialism with a philosophical antimodernism and ethnic chauvinism and thought of this political philosophy as the way to think through our ability to resist the growing dominion of technology, one cannot but recoil in horror at the realisation that Heidegger ultimately never fully relinquished at least some version of the disastrous views he held in the 1930s.

In terms of Heidegger's antisemitism, this is a difficult and sensitive issue. There have been a lot of knee-jerk responses to individual passages, which would appear to incriminate Heidegger, which certain acolytes in turn continue to try to explain away and contextualise. Some of the attempts to redeem Heidegger in the face of overwhelming evidence are quite extraordinary and betoken a kind of blind devotion that really doesn't serve any function in honest intellectual discussion. At the same time, the reactionary cheap shots are rather unhelpful in their own right. Whatever way we want to try to qualify Heidegger's antisemitism, however, we simply cannot ignore the fact that he harboured and sometimes expressed views which simply must be condemned. As it turns out, for this reader at least, Heidegger cannot really articulate a coherent political philosophy, owing in part to the fact that his philosophy doesn't really admit to being employed in the manner in which he wants to use it, but that is not something one can simply presume; after all, it was Heidegger himself who tried to combine his politics with his philosophy. Granted, Heidegger is quite critical of rivalling attempts to offer a National Socialist political philosophy or political science. Indeed, Heidegger becomes more and more critical of aspects of National Socialism as time goes by.[8] However, regardless of how one wants to engage in apologetics or semantics here, the fact remains that Heidegger believed that only through the marriage of his philosophy with the cultural and spiritual awakening of the German people that he identified in Nazism, could Europe survive the planetary crisis brought on by the history of the oblivion of being. In his own retrospective on his rectorate, for example, we find Heidegger openly admitting, as he did again in his interview with *Der Spiegel* in 1966:

> I saw in the movement that had gained power the possibility of an inner recollection and renewal of the people and a path that would allow it to discover its historical vocation in the Western world. I believed that, renewing itself, the university might also be called to contribute to this inner self-collection of the people, providing it with a measure. ('The Rectorate', 483)

Heidegger's *Black Notebooks* have, as mentioned, been the subject of heated controversy ever since their immanent publication was announced, and, among other things, they provide a fascinating insight into the personality of Heidegger. He was a spectacularly arrogant and pretentious human being, a person riddled with jealousy and bitterness. He became increasingly disillusioned with academia in Germany and was clearly devastated not to have had more of an impact in his first and only attempt to enter the political fray as the Nazi rector of Freiburg University. For those who believed that we would find incontrovertible proof of a level of antisemitism that went beyond anything we could previously have associated with Heidegger, the notebooks may prove somewhat underwhelming. Richard Polt collated every reference in the first three volumes to Jews, Jewishness, the Jewish people, and, of the fifteen or so explicit references, only a few of them are genuinely troublesome and don't really add anything more to our knowledge of Heidegger's antisemitism than what was already available.[9] Of the three volumes of the *Black Notebooks* initially published, there is no evidence of any antisemitism in the first volume. The problems begin in volume 95, which was translated into English recently. Again, though a number of Heidegger's remarks here are deeply problematic, it is very misleading to present these notebooks as the intellectual diary of a rabid antisemite. Heidegger's criticisms of and reservations concerning National Socialism far outweigh the sporadic remarks concerning Jews. Nevertheless, they do confirm what the available evidence already indicated, that Heidegger was an antisemite and that he believed he could articulate his political views and his racist prejudices from within the framework of his philosophy.

Towards the end of the Second World War, Heidegger appears to have fallen badly out of favour with the Nazi authorities. He had been snubbed on a number of occasions after he stepped down as rector of Freiburg University, being conspicuously omitted from the German delegation to attend an international philosophy conference in Paris. Heidegger further reports that his books were banned from being sold and could only be purchased by certain booksellers using plain covers with no identifying marks. Heidegger further alleges that the authorities had planted spies to report back on his lectures and that toward the end of the war he was placed in the most expendable category of academics and put to work digging trenches as part of the war effort.[10] As the Allied forces approached Freiburg, the philosophy faculty fled to the hills outside the city and conducted some academic activities within the grounds of the castle of their host. This was a period of great uncertainty and upheaval for everyone; for Heidegger, it was to prove even more complicated still, since he was, by this point, in the midst of another love affair with a woman who had begun taking his classes in Freiburg in 1942.[11]

NOTES

1. Heidegger makes a number of positive remarks about both Hitler and *Mein Kampf* in letters to his brother Fritz and sent him a copy of the book as a Christmas present in 1931.
2. Julius Streicher was the founder and publisher of one of the most abhorrent sources of antisemitic propaganda in Nazi Germany—a newspaper called *Der Stürmer*. Streicher was tried and convicted during the Nuremburg trials after the end of the Second World War and was executed in 1946.
3. Herbert Marcuse, Hans Jonas, and Karl Löwith, for example, were never able to bring themselves to forgive Heidegger. Marcuse's letters to Heidegger after the war attest to his frustration and dismay at his former teacher's political attitudes. See *The Heidegger Controversy: A Critical Reader* (see Marcuse, 1993, 160–64).
4. Ott quotes from some of Husserl's correspondence in 1933: 'Before this he [Heidegger] broke off all relations with me (and very soon after his appointment) and in recent years has allowed his antisemitism to come increasingly to the fore, even in his dealings with his group of devoted Jewish students and his Faculty colleagues' (Ott, 1993, 185).
5. For my own part I can't quite see how it took the appearance of the notorious *Black Notebooks* to convince many Heideggerians that there were serious problems to be faced in terms of the relationship between Heidegger's philosophy and his political views. He had already made it abundantly clear to Löwith in 1936 that his political views were based directly on key concepts in *Being and Time*. What is more—he vigorously looked to articulate a political philosophy, based on core concepts from within his thought, throughout the 1930s and in ways that he didn't fully abandon even after the Second World War.
6. A good example of this is Derrida's interview which was published in the first edition of Richard Wolin's critical reader on the controversy (see Derrida, 1991).
7. Typically, Heidegger's discussion of *Gelassenheit* (releasement) as the appropriate comportment for a thinking that could respond to the particular challenges facing humanity in the technological age is seen as uncontroversial and, further, as Heidegger's renunciation of the valourisation of the will which was an integral part of his support for National Socialism. Where the early Heidegger championed the resolve to will, the later Heidegger, who is moving away from this early voluntarism, favours a quietistic, zen-like 'releasement' from the will. This is a false dichotomy and one which Heidegger frequently rejects in his self-interpretations. Moreover, in the 'Memorial Address', where the notion of *Gelassenheit* comes to the fore, Heidegger repeatedly invokes the notion of *Bodenständigkeit* (rootedness or autochthony) and the importance of the German people once again finding a way to become rooted in the native soil of their

homeland in such a way that great works of German art can again flourish from out of this Germanic rootedness. This is a highly controversial and problematic aspect of Heidegger's confrontation with modernity, not least given the ignominy of the association of *Bodenständigkeit* with the *Blut und Boden* rhetoric of Nazi regime.

8. It is also worth bearing in mind that Heidegger's tenure as rector lasted less than a year and he quickly fell out of favour with the Nazi authorities owing in many ways to the incommensurability of Heidegger's own idiosyncratic political vision and the official Nazi policies, which he wasn't always keen to implement.

9. That is not to say that the notebooks do not confirm some of our worst fears about Heidegger's attempts to defend or offer a philosophical justification for his political views and his ethnic chauvinism. And scholars such as Trawny are keen to show how Heidegger was trying to inscribe antisemitism into his being-historical thinking. However, much of what Heidegger wants to do in these passages is an extension of and elaboration of moves he makes elsewhere.

10. In his interview with *Der Spiegel*, Heidegger recalls, 'In the last year of the war, 500 of the most important scholars [*Wissenschaftler*] and artists of every kind were exempted from war service. I was not among the exempted. On the contrary, in the summer of 1944 I was ordered to work on the fortifications on the Rhine' ('Only a God Can Save Us', 102–3).

11. Princess Margot von Sachsen-Meiningen had been a student of Heidegger's and they developed a close and longstanding relationship. Heidegger spent prolonged periods with Margot and her children in a lodge she had moved into around 1944. Heidegger apparently found himself torn between his wife and his lover in the immediate aftermath of the war, and this stress may have contributed to the nervous breakdown he suffered around this time.

SEVEN
Return from Syracuse

The initial years following the end of the war were turbulent for Heidegger. This was a period of great hardship for many Germans, so it is difficult to muster too much sympathy for the one-time Nazi, especially when one hears him again insist on the importance of the native soil of the homeland for German art and philosophy in a public address in his hometown of Messkirch in 1955. Nevertheless, for Heidegger this was to prove a trying time. He found himself in the academic wilderness, banned from teaching, while he and his wife had to endure the uncertainty of their sons' fates, both of whom languished in prison camps on the Eastern front.

At one point during the denazification proceedings, the committee reviewing Heidegger's case threatened to confiscate his private library, and it was this possibility in particular which appears to have led to his complete mental breakdown.[1] He was treated in a sanatorium and eventually began to recover. Five years after his dramatic fall from grace, Heidegger was reinstated at the university and resumed teaching. However, the stigma and questions concerning his Nazi past haunted Heidegger for the rest of his life. Notwithstanding, Heidegger's productivity during the late 1940s and into the 1950s was quite remarkable. He began to focus on issues concerning language, poetry and technology, all the time returning to the question concerning the meaning of being, the concomitant posture of *Gelassenheit* (Releasement) and the notion of 'appropriation' or 'enownment' (*Ereignis*)[2] which he had begun to introduce as a key concept in his thinking in the mid-1930s.

There is no denying that stylistically it is almost impossible to imagine that the author of *Being and Time* could also pen some of the essays and lectures from the 1950s and 1960s. Again, the tendency here has been to conflate this change or shift in language with the notion of 'the turn' itself, which, as we mentioned previously, has led to some not unproblematic interpretations.

TECHNOLOGY

Some of the central philosophical preoccupations of Heidegger's later thinking revolve around questions concerning the role that technology plays in our lives, questions already beginning to emerge as early as *Being and Time*. One prevailing misapprehension among critics of Heidegger is the belief that his work on technology is simply a symptom of his provincialism and antimodernism, which is then diagnosed as yet another example of the disastrous mind-set that Heidegger succumbed to along with a generation of post-Weimar German intellectuals. However, this does great disservice to some of Heidegger's most important philosophical work after *Being and Time*. Heidegger is concerned about the increasing level of mechanisation and technology in the middle of the twentieth century, and for this reason, it should come as no surprise that a lot of his descriptions and ideas are similar to and influenced by the work of writers such as Oswald Spengler and Ernst Jünger. However, these are in many ways only *superficial affinities,* since Heidegger begins to look at the technological age in terms of his unique history of the forgetting or oblivion of being. Heidegger is returning to his unusual and provocative story concerning the history of the unfolding of the metaphysical epochs that have held sway in Western metaphysics.

In 1949, while still banned from teaching, Heidegger delivered a series of lectures at the Bremen Club.[3] Heidegger now attempts to systematically tackle what he took to be the defining features of the modern technological age. Some of Heidegger's insights and analyses here are among his finest philosophical achievements and certainly give the lie to the idea that his work after *Being and Time* pales philosophically in comparison with his early masterpiece.[4] To be fair, Heideggerians generally don't dismiss Heidegger's later work, but there is a belief at times among non-specialists that Heidegger's early work is philosophically more respectable than some of the more obscure later work. The lectures themselves, as indicated by the titles, focus on a number of related themes including *Das Ding* (The Thing), *Das Gestell* (Enframing, or Positionality), *Die Gefahr* (The Danger) and *Die Kehre* (The Turning). Heidegger reworked and crafted these fascinating discussions into what is one of his finest short essays, 'The Question Concerning Technology'. In the published essay, Heidegger manages to distil some of the central features of his thought, and it stands today as the single most important philosophical piece of work on some of the issues concerning the technological age we live in.

The essay has been dogged by a certain amount of controversy ever since the publication of the Bremen lectures revealed a number of statements by Heidegger which appear to address the Holocaust but in a manner, which has been roundly condemned by commentators. We can turn briefly to the remarks themselves (and the underlying context) before summarising Heidegger's basic position with respect to technology, in particular the essence of the technological age which Heidegger cryptically declares to be 'nothing technological'.

In the course of one of the lectures Heidegger makes a remark which has taken on a life of its own in the Heidegger controversy. It is referred to, rather unhelpfully, as the 'Agriculture Remark':

> Agriculture is now a mechanised food industry, in essence the same as the production of corpses in the gas chambers and extermination camps, the same as the blockading and starving of countries, the same as the production of hydrogen bombs. (BFL, 27)

Taken out of context, this is a bizarre statement, and numerous commentators, some with a dubious polemical agenda, have used this comment to castigate Heidegger and condemn the gross inadequacy of such a response to the Holocaust. However, once one places this remark back into the context of the lecture and Heidegger's subsequent published essay, it becomes clear that he is trying to address a number of related issues from the standpoint of the way in which they have been influenced or determined by the essence of modern technology.

The essence of modern technology, Heidegger will conclude, is the *Gestell*. Even though the word *Gestell* would ordinarily mean something like a frame, a bookcase or picture frame, William Lovitt chose to translate the word with the slightly cumbersome term 'Enframing'. For Heidegger, the term has a wider meaning than the notion of a frame, and he is certainly not suggesting that technology 'frames' things in the sense of placing them in a picture frame. In more recent years, some Heidegger scholars have favoured the term 'positionality' as a more apt translation of the term. One can only presume that this is because they want to draw attention to the manner in which Heidegger emphasises the verb *stellen* (to put or to position) in his discussion of modern technology's essence. However, the problem is that Heidegger also chose a word which had other connotations besides 'positionality' and, as such, the term Enframing is equally if not more suitable as a translation.

The point of Heidegger's remark is not to conflate the Holocaust with the harvesting of grain, as some commentators have suggested, nor is Heidegger guilty of some kind of category error in treating current agricultural methods as morally equivalent to genocide. Heidegger is *not* arguing that genocide is no different morally from agriculture or armed conflict. Rather, Heidegger is interested in the role that the essence of technology plays in the way genocide was undertaken during the Second World War or the manner in which nineteenth-century agricultural practices and animal husbandry have given way to factory farming. Part of what Heidegger is interested in, then, is the role that the essence of technology (Enframing) has played in the way everything including genocide, war and agriculture has taken place in the twentieth century. Failure to discern this intention has led to widespread condemnation and vilification of Heidegger.

Another controversial remark that Heidegger makes during one of the lectures that he did not in fact deliver at the time, amounts to an attempt to condemn what happened to the inmates in the death camps. This troublesome passage also needs to be connected with his concerns with the role of *Gestell* in the technological age:

> Are there times when we could have noticed *the* distress, the dominance of distresslessness? There are indications. Only we do not attend to them.
>
> Hundreds of thousands die in masses. Do they die? They perish. They are put down. Do they die? They become pieces of inventory of a standing reserve for the fabrication of corpses. Do they die? They are unobtrusively liquidated in annihilation camps. And even apart from such as these—millions now in China abjectly end in starvation.
>
> To die, however, means to carry out death in its essence. To be able to die means to be capable of carrying this out. We are only capable of it, however, when our essence is endeared to the essence of death. (BFL, 53)

Heidegger is revisiting his *Being and Time* account of authentic death here and suggesting that what has been stripped from the victims in the death camps is their freedom, that is, their freedom-towards-death,[5] and that this has been effected in particular through the levelling ordinances of Enframing. Of course, this does not explain *why* the Nazis attempted genocide; rather, it is Heidegger's attempt to focus on a particular aspect of that genocide which, he believed, was an important feature of the technological age. The Nazi genocide bore all the hallmarks of the influence of Enframing: people were reduced to stock, number, item, resource and ultimately waste to be disposed of.[6]

Leaving the controversial features of the lectures to one side and returning to the published essay, one could say that, all things considered, 'The Question Concerning Technology' is a good place to begin for someone trying to come to grips with Heidegger for the first time, since he manages to distil his entire philosophical vision in this difficult yet rewarding essay. His views concerning equipmentality, publicness, *das Man*,[7] the manner in which being comes to have meaning and the epochal way that this occurs are all deployed in Heidegger's attempt to come to grips with what he takes to be the essence of the technological age.

Heidegger is interested in the essence of modern technology and wants to try to find a 'free' relationship to that essence. This in itself is a hint as to the nature of our current relationship to modern technology which Heidegger will argue is not, in fact, a free relationship, nor is modern technology something that we are in charge or control of in the ways we might suppose.

One way of understanding Heidegger's views on technology is to reconsider some of the insights he developed in *Being and Time*. In that work, Heidegger notices that our ordinary, everyday way of existing is such that we are utterly dependent upon equipment, a concept he understands very broadly to include all the tools, implements, devices we use, even the most elementary, such as a walking stick. Consider how your own day began before you picked up this book; or perhaps you are already reading this text on a Kindle or some such device. For most of us, the day probably began with an electronic alarm of some kind. Many of us can probably identify some fairly major changes in terms of this particular type of equipment. As a child, most of the bedrooms in my grandparents' houses had rather rudimentary alarm clocks—ones that needed to be wound regularly in order to keep time. I still remember distinctly the fanfare that greeted the arrival of radio-alarm clocks and my own excitement at receiving one of these clunky contraptions. Today, many of us begin our day with the sound of our smartphone beeping or buzzing. While still in bed, we might check our messages on WhatsApp, Viber or Facebook; after that we might be tempted to have a quick peek at our work e-mails before scanning the headlines or the sports pages on some website or other. We then get out of bed and, depending on the time of year, we turn on the light, head to the bathroom, turn on the lights and fan, use the electric shower, brush our teeth, perhaps with an electric toothbrush. Once dressed, we go to the kitchen, open the refrigerator to retrieve some chilled goods, put bread in the electric toaster, turn on the electric kettle or perhaps the electric coffee maker. For many people, the television in the kitchen has already been turned on; some listen to the morning radio, while others scan their smartphones, tablets or notebooks in search of news, weather and the like.

Many of you will have left the house and driven to work or else used some form of public transport to get to your place of work or study. In the case of academics and students, we arrive at offices and classes, turn on computers and laptops; if we are lecturing, we have memory sticks to use in interactive classrooms for PowerPoint presentations; we have perhaps printed our lecture notes along with handouts for the students. After our classes we return to our offices, the students go to the library or another class, or perhaps to a canteen or a coffee shop where they can purchase food and drinks, all of which have been produced, preserved and delivered using all manner of networks of equipment. In my case, I turn on the light in my office, switch on my desktop computer and begin reading and responding to e-mails; the office phone might ring, and I can field messages on my smartphone as well. I submit attendance records electronically and upload documents and links onto student webpages. If I still have some time left over, I open a document I have been working on. Today, I have opened the document which will eventually be published as a print book or made available to you on the electronic reading device you are holding in your hand right now—but only after it has been submitted as an attachment to an e-mail and then sent back and forth between a copyeditor and me with electronically tracked changes and revisions. Eventually, a final, corrected version is attached by another e-mail from me to the copyeditor and is typeset electronically before eventually it is ready to be published. The more and more we begin to examine our everyday world, the more we realise that our environment is completely saturated with technological equipment that we use automatically in order to facilitate our various projects and ends.

In *Being and Time*, there are hints that Heidegger was beginning to worry about some of these developments insofar as the equipmental, mechanistic nature of our everyday world was actually changing the manner in which that world revealed itself to us or, more to the point, was indicative of a world revealing itself to us in very unusual and, for Heidegger, alarming ways. He notes in his 1927 masterpiece that when we look at a wood, for example, we no longer see a wood but instead a source of timber ready for harvest. Similarly, we often regard mountains as resources to be mined or used: the mountain is a quarry of rock (BT, 100). If we then consider the ways in which Heidegger characterises our typical, public, inauthentic existence and his concomitant suspicion of mass society and mass media, we can begin to see how these various strands can be spun together into some of the central threads that become the fabric of 'The Question Concerning Technology'. Granted, Heidegger has not quite developed the insights and views that he was to develop in the 1940s and 1950s, but it is clear that Heidegger's thinking about technology was there in embryonic form in *Being and Time*.

Moreover, some of Heidegger's insights are remarkably prophetic. If we consider the manner in which we have come to rely on laptops, smartphones and tablets these days, we might well wonder how it is that we ever managed without them. And yet, I myself had already finished my BA in Ireland before I had an e-mail account. I didn't own a laptop until my second year as a PhD student in Boston. Indeed, as a final year undergraduate student in Ireland in the late 1990s, I submitted most of my essays and term papers handwritten, with the exception of my final year thesis. Even the manner in which we keep social engagements or make plans has now changed to the point that it is almost inconceivable to people that we just arrange a date, time and place in advance, and everyone keeps to the plan and shows up on time. Instead we make provisional plans, which we frequently revise or amend via text or messaging services. People think nothing of arriving later than originally agreed so long as they have alerted the others by text or instant message. What it means to 'be' in any and all walks of life has been greatly affected; what it means to be a student, for example, appears to be changing radically, and the same could be said of what it means to 'be' a teacher, a writer, a doctor, a musician. The world begins to reveal itself very differently to us than it did to, say, a farmer living in rural Germany in the 1800s. We can think of examples closer to home. Consider just how incompetent or ill-adept many elderly people seem to be with the rudiments of what many of us take to be part and parcel of our quotidian existence. I cannot even begin to imagine how bizarre and unrecognisable my own grandparents would find what 'we' take to be commonplace. Two of them were already dead before there was any mention of the internet, and another had died before I even knew it existed. And yet, I lived in the same 'world' as my grandparents for a significant stretch of time, the last, my grandmother, dying in 2010. Nevertheless, my Grandmother was already clearly out of place, where once she confidently navigated her way around a 'world' within which she commanded respect for her efficiency and competence. Somehow, the world my extended family now occupy has changed drastically, and yet I never noticed it happening. It just seemed to be the case without anyone having decided that we would live differently.

Recently I visited my father's birthplace in North County Cork, where now my cousin trains racehorses from stables on the old farm. My grandfather had cultivated an interest in racehorses and began to breed his own thoroughbreds in the early 1930s, around the time that he would have registered the family colours. If he were suddenly to reappear today, just over twenty years after his passing, there is much he would recognise, and much that has changed would not be that surprising, since these would be the kinds of changes that any of us would associate with the passing of time. These are simply the ways that things change and progress and decline in the course of a lifetime. My grandfather would recognise many of the old buildings, and he would understand many of the new ones. They would make sense. The new racing and exercise gallops and horse boxes would make sense, as would many of the vehicles. He might even recognise the current incarnations of my first cousin and me, different as we are from the fresh-faced teens that said goodbye to him.

But imagine his puzzlement if one of us produced a smartphone and began to look up information about the sire of a horse we were discussing. We might then decide to watch the finish of one of the sire's races on the same device. Or we might decide to watch video footage of the work that a horse had recently completed on the gallops. We might throw the footage up onto the television screen. No sign of studbooks, form guides, racing newspapers, racing calendars: everything simply available at the touch of a button. Perhaps my grandfather would wistfully recall a horse race from his youth and begin to recount to us the drama that unfolded, an event that for him had no other testimony apart from what survived in his own memory. Now all of a sudden, we locate footage of the race on YouTube, and he is able to relive everything again, courtesy of our living room's flat-screen TV and surround-sound speakers. Imagine how amazed he might be to find himself suddenly enjoying a video chat with one of his grandchildren or great-grandchildren in another country. Any and all of these innovations and facilities are commonplace to us, but we might find ourselves having to explain an endless array of changes and developments to someone who has not been here for the last twenty years.

Heidegger makes a key observation: that all of these almost imperceptible yet nevertheless radical changes are not the outcome of a decision or series of decisions made by a person or a collective. As he writes in the 'Memorial Address',

> No single man, no group of men, no commission of prominent statesmen, scientists, and technicians, no conference of leaders of commerce and industry, can brake or direct the progress of history in the atomic age. No merely human organisation is capable of gaining dominion over it. (DT, 52)

For Heidegger, the essence of technology is nothing technological, and part of what he means by this is that what is going on here happens at the level of metaphysics. The way beings 'present' themselves to us is now happening in a different way because we are in a new epoch in the history of the metaphysics of presence. The way everything appears to us is now filtered through the essence of modern technology, that is, Enframing.

In terms of the history of the metaphysics of presence, in every era or epoch beings tend to be rendered or reveal themselves as present in particular, trademark ways. For this reason, some commentators describe Heidegger's story of the unfolding of Western metaphysics as an attempt to illustrate the various 'Gestalts' of the metaphysics of presence since the time of Plato, culminating in the complete victory of the metaphysics of presence in the era of Enframing, where Enframing can be understood as the Gestalt of the technological age.

So, what exactly is unique or different about the way things are revealed to us through Enframing compared to a previous era which also had technological devices and equipment after its own fashion, such as crossbows and telegraphs? In every epoch, everything is governed, in terms of the way beings came to presence, by a certain manner of revealing. Things become apparent to us as what we take them to be in the nexus of meaningful things. The difference, for Heidegger, is the *way* that everything is revealed in the age of modern technology. Heidegger refers to Enframing as a 'challenging revealing' in which everything everywhere is reduced to a resource to be used or waste to be disposed of: beings are *challenged* to reveal themselves as fitting into the Enframing in this way. We can see the symptoms of this almost everywhere, especially in how we have exploited the planet as essentially a giant gasoline station since the early part of the twentieth century:

> The world now appears as an object open to the attacks of calculative thought, attacks that nothing is believed able any longer to resist. Nature becomes a gigantic gasoline station, an energy source for modern technology and industry. The relation of man to the world as such, in principle a technical one, developed in the seventeenth century first and only in Europe. . . . The power concealed in modern technology determines the relation of man to that which exists. It rules the whole earth. Indeed, already man is beginning to advance beyond the earth into outer space. (DT, 50)

At bottom, Heidegger is not talking about technological equipment or devices in or of themselves, then. He is more concerned with the way the world, along with everything and everyone in it, is revealed to us such that we only seem to understand anything through the lens of Enframing. If we think, for example, of one of the most celebrated intellectuals of recent decades, the late theoretical physicist and cosmologist Stephen Hawking, we can begin to appreciate just how prescient some of Heidegger's concerns were. A few years ago, Hawking pronounced philosophy 'dead' in a way that I think Heidegger would see as symptomatic of this more general problem. In *The Grand Design*, Hawking looks to defend his version of the 'M-theory' (a form of model realism):

> Each universe has many possible histories and many possible states at later times, that is, at times like the present, long after their creation. Most of these states would be quite unlike the universe we observe and quite unsuitable for the existence of any form of life. Only a very few would allow creatures like us to exist. Thus our presence selects out from this vast array only those universes that are compatible with our existence. Although we are puny and insignificant on the scale of the cosmos, this makes us in a sense the lords of creation. (Hawking and Mlodinow, 2010, 9)

Already here, we can see how some of Heidegger's claims concerning the dangers inherent in the essence of modern technology might be brought to bear against Hawking's scientistic arrogance. Having already proclaimed philosophy 'dead', since it does not automatically conform to the concerns of contemporary physicists, he goes on to suggest that the universe is best understood from the standpoint of human beings conceived as 'the lords of creation'. Consider as a response Heidegger's prophetic claim some sixty years previous concerning the manner in which human beings would become more and more constrained by the eliminative outlook of Enframing:

> Yet when destining reigns in the mode of Enframing, it is the supreme danger. This danger attests itself to us in two ways. As soon as what is unconcealed no longer conceals man even as object, but does so, rather, exclusively as standing reserve, and man in the midst of the objectlessness is nothing but the ordered of the standing-reserve, then he comes to the very brink of a precipitous fall; that is, he comes to the point where he himself will have to be taken as standing-reserve. Meanwhile man, precisely as the one so threatened, exalts himself to the posture of the lord of the earth. In this way the impression comes to prevail that everything man encounters exists only insofar as it his construct. This illusion gives rise in turn to one final delusion: it seems as though man everywhere and always encounters only himself. Heisenberg has with complete correctness pointed out that the real must present itself to contemporary man in this way. *In truth, however, precisely nowhere does man today any longer encounter himself, i.e., his essence.* (QCT, 27)

If one thinks of Hawking's previous theoretical aspirations, one can see where Heidegger might take issue. Hawking was once an ardent supporter of the quest for a 'theory of everything'. That is not to say that such attempts are of necessity wrongheaded. The problem is that those engaged in such undertakings are sometimes prone to the view that anything that does not come under the umbrella of their investigations is somehow meaningless, irrelevant, or simply absurd. The great delusion at the heart of this asphyxiating, eliminative approach is the idea, then, that anything that doesn't contribute to this attempt is obsolete, unnecessary, folk psychological, romantic, anachronistic, what have you. Granted, Hawking eventually lost confidence in the possibility of a single, unifying theory of everything. However, the fact remains that Hawking himself was enslaved to the idea that *everything* must ultimately be explained in terms of physics and mathematics for it to be in any way useful or significant—or, indeed, simply to count as *being*. What Hawking overlooks, Heidegger might argue, is the hidden prejudice governing the manner in which he thinks the world and the universe must be revealed or interpreted, which is, ultimately, in a painfully constricted way. When did we decide that the *only* way of investigating or describing what was relevant in terms of understanding life and the world around us was through the language of physics or mathematics and the rather limited scope they allow for in terms of understanding something? Not only that, why would we assume that everything within the cosmos and whatever it means for it to be is something that simply reduces to whatever paradigmatic (and most likely flawed and provisional) scientific model happens to be in vogue right now? Is this not precisely the great arrogance and indeed the great delusion that Heidegger warns against in the previous passage?

One can track a similar development in the philosophy of mind and cognitive science over the last decades. It became more or less standard to refer to the mind or brain as a machine, a computer, a central processing unit and so on. Granted, these are only metaphors, and many theorists working in this field are gifted philosophers in their own right, ranking among some of the brightest names the discipline has produced over the last few decades. Nevertheless, the choice of metaphor itself is not entirely neutral or innocent. Things reveal themselves to us now, as technological devices or equipment to be understood or analysed, fixed or programmed according to principles which belong to a different field entirely. It rarely seems to occur to many practitioners that if they begin by treating the mind or brain as something *like* a computer or machine, the results of their analyses and experiments in turn will most likely be determined, if not indeed skewed, in ways which have more to do with the metaphors being used than the mind or brain itself. Merleau-Ponty, in his last published essay, characterises the methodology and procedure of contemporary science in ways which very much resonate with some of Heidegger's descriptions in 'The Question Concerning Technology'. And the nature of the criticism seems clear: if you treat nature as something which should be described through mathematical physics, for example, then you will end up with descriptions of nature which are in accord with mathematical physics. Merleau-Ponty's description of this scientific wrongheadedness is rather elegant and bears repeating:

> Today more than ever, science is sensitive to intellectual fads and fashions. When a model has succeeded in one order of problems, it is tried out everywhere else. At the present time, for example, our embryology and biology are full of 'gradients.' Just how these differ from what classical tradition called 'order' or 'totality' is not at all clear. This question, however, is not raised: it is not even allowed. The gradient is a net we throw out to sea, without knowing what we will haul back in it. It is a slender twig upon which unforeseeable crystalisations will form. No doubt this freedom of operation will serve well to overcome many a pointless dilemma—provided from time to time we take stock, and ask ourselves why the apparatus works in one place and fails in others. For all its flexibility, science must understand itself; it must see itself as a construction based on a brute, existent world and not claim for its blind operations the constitutive value that 'concepts of nature' were granted in a certain idealist philosophy. To say that the world is, by nominal definition, the object x of our operations is to treat scientist's knowledge as if it were absolute, as if everything that is and has been was meant only to enter the laboratory. Thinking 'operationally' has become a sort of absolute artificialism, such as we see in the ideology of cybernetics, where human creations are derived from a natural information process, itself conceived on the model of human machines. If this kind of thinking were to extend its dominion over humanity and history; and if, ignoring what we know of them through contact and our own situations, it were to set out to construct them on the basis of a few abstract indices (as a decadent psychoanalysis and culturalism have done in the United States)—then, since the human being truly becomes the *manipulandum* he thinks he is, we enter into a cultural regimen in which there is neither truth nor falsehood concerning humanity and history, into a sleep, or nightmare from which there is no awakening. (Merleau-Ponty, 1993, 122)

Merleau-Ponty wants to restore scientific thinking to the path and place from which it should take its bearings, which, means a return to phenomenological analysis:

> Scientific thinking, a thinking which looks on from above, and thinks of the object-in-general, must return to the 'there is' which precedes it; to the site, the soil of the sensible and humanly modified world such as it is in our lives and for our bodies—not that possible body which we may legitimately think of as an information machine but this actual body I call mine, this sentinel standing quietly at the command of my words and my acts. Further, *associated bodies* must be revived along with my body—'others',

not merely as my congeners, as the zoologist says, but others who haunt me and whom I haunt; 'others' along with whom I haunt a single, present, and actual Being as no animal ever haunted those of his own species, territory, or habitat. In this primordial historicity, science's agile and improvisatory thought will learn to ground itself upon things themselves and upon itself, and will once more become philosophy. (Merleau-Ponty, 1993, 122–23)

If we take a more straightforward example, perhaps we can bring the point into sharper focus: suppose we are watching a performance of a Shakespearean play or a famous opera, or we are listening to an orchestra perform one of Beethoven's symphonies. Now, there is no question but that one of the ways that we *could* describe each of these events is through the language of mathematics or physics. However, is it really the case that any of us would further conclude that these were *exhaustive* explanations? Suppose someone feels intense grief as a result of a tragedy, a bereavement or perhaps the end of a relationship. Would we be so quick to concede ground to someone who described everything at the level of neurochemistry and then insisted that they had offered exhaustive explanations? And yet, something like this prejudice is beginning to hold more and more sway in terms of the way everything about our lives is interpreted and understood. The acme of this tendency then can be seen to be Hawking's myopic understanding of what philosophy entails in its attempt to reveal what makes meaning possible in our lives. This helps explain Heidegger's invocation of René Char in his 1966 interview with *Der Spiegel*. Heidegger responds to his interviewers concerning the role that technology plays in contemporary life in the following way:

> This is no longer the earth on which man lives. As you know, I recently had a long conversation with Rene Char of the Provence, the poet and resistance fighter. Rocket bases are being built in the Provence and the country is being devastated in an incredible way. The poet, who certainly cannot be suspected of sentimentality and of glorification of the idyllic, tells me that the uprooting of man which is taking place there will be the end, if poetry and thought do not once more succeed to a position of might without force. ('Only a God Can Save Us', 106)

At first glance, this reference to the importance of poetry might seem a rather strange response from someone who is speaking about what he takes to be a planetary crisis of technology. However, Heidegger's point relates to the eliminative character of the metaphysical Gestalt governing the way beings come to presence in the age of modern technology. What needs to happen is for other forms of revealing—for example—poetry, to once again allow people to see things coming to presence in ways other than what is rather aggressively demanded by Enframing. How this could or would happen is never obvious. As the ultimate aspiration would be to overcome what Heidegger takes to be the final epoch in the history of the metaphysics of presence, this is *not* going to be the 'achievement' of any person or group of individuals, anymore than Enframing's revelation of everyone and everything as resources is a consequence of the aims or the intentions of any individual or group. Nevertheless, we can begin to appreciate the fact that the only way that anything *can* actually *be* meaningfully present or manifest is through the human being. While what threatens us in terms of the ultimate dominion of the essence of technology is the greatest danger of all, the fact that this dominion can only happen in tandem with the disclosive capacities and activities of human beings means that it is at the same time the 'saving power'.[8]

In subsequent work, Heidegger will begin to describe the appropriate comportment of human beings (*Gelassenheit*). We cannot control the manner in which things are meaningfully present and at the same time 'are' such that they can only appear as meaningfully present to and through us. The term Heidegger uses is *Gelassenheit*, which is typically translated as 'releasement'. Whereas Heidegger's earlier notion of *Entschlossenheit* (Resoluteness) is typically criticised as being too voluntaristic, the later notion, *Gelassenheit*, is rejected as too quietistic.

In an essay sometimes understood as Heidegger's attempt finally to pronounce dead the project of *Being and Time*, he returns to the ideas we have been sketching earlier:

> Thus we are bound to the characterisation of Being as presencing. It derives its binding force from the beginning of the unconcealment of Being as something that can be said, that is, can be thought. Ever since the beginning of Western thinking with the Greeks, all saying of 'Being' and 'Is' is held in the remembrance of the determination of Being and presencing which is binding for thinking. This holds true of the thinking that directs the most modern technology and industry, though by now only in a certain sense. Now that modern technology has arranged its expansion and rule over the whole earth, it is not just the sputniks and their by-products that are circling around our planet; it is rather

> Being as presencing in the sense of calculable material that claims all the inhabitants of the earth in a uniform manner. (OTB, 6–7)

Heidegger continues with his efforts to track the history of the epochs of Western metaphysics and the manner in which the oblivion of being is characteristic of that history:

> The history of Being means the destiny of Being in whose sendings both the sending and the 'It' which sends forth hold back with their self-manifestation. To hold back is, in Greek, *epoche*. Hence, we speak of the epochs of the destiny of Being. Epoch does not mean here a span of time in occurrence, but rather the fundamental characteristic of sending, the actual holding-back of itself in favour of the gift, that is, of Being with regard to the grounding of Beings. . . . The epochs overlap each other in their sequence so that the original sending of Being as presence is more and more obscured in different ways. Only the gradual removal of these obscuring covers—that is what is meant by 'dismantling'—procures for thinking a preliminary insight into what then reveals itself as the destiny of Being. Because one everywhere represents the destiny of Being only as history, and history only as a kind of occurrence, one tries in vain to interpret this occurrence in terms of what was said in *Being and Time* about the historicity of man (Dasein) (not of Being). By contrast, the only possible way to anticipate the latter thought on the destiny of Being from the perspective of *Being and Time* is to think through what was presented in *Being and Time* about the dismantling of the ontological doctrine of the Being of beings. (OTB, 9)

With respect to the unique role of human beings, Heidegger reaffirms a point he has been trying to make for the greater part of his career:

> For it might be that what distinguishes man as man is determined precisely by what we must think about here: man, who is concerned with and approached by presence, who, through being thus approached, is himself present in his own way for all present and absent beings. Man: standing within the approach of presence, but in such a way that he receives as a gift the presencing that It gives by perceiving what appears in letting-presence. If man were not the constant of the gift given by the 'It gives presence', if that which is extended in the gift did not reach man, then not only would human being remain concealed in the absence of this gift, not only closed off, but man would remain excluded from the scope of: It gives Being. Man would not be man. (OTB, 12)

Heidegger remains concerned with the levelling influence of Enframing in the technological age for the rest of his life and sees the chief task of thinking to be one of finding a way of responding to the increasing technicity and mechanisation that dominate how we understand everything, including ourselves. This leads Heidegger to increase his focus on language and poetry along with the enigmatic notion *Gelassenheit*.[9] Heidegger experiments further with style and attempts to employ the dialogue form in some of his best-known discussions of *Gelassenheit*. In the words of some of the interlocutors operating as thinly disguised fronts for Heidegger's ideas (or indeed foils to be confuted), we do have some valuable resources that allow us to analyse Heidegger's views concerning *Gelassenheit* as the appropriate response for thinking in the technological age.

NOTES

1. Relatively little is known of Heidegger's breakdown in the mid-1940s. In his biography, Safranski summarises what seems to be known about this period as follows: 'Heidegger in fact had a physical and mental breakdown in the spring of 1946 and underwent psychosomatic treatment by Victor Baron von Gebsattel, a physician and psychologist of the Binswanger school of Dasein analysis, a psychoanalytical method that had been inspired by Heidegger's philosophy, whose practitioners included Heidegger's later friend Medard Boss. Heidegger's own information on his breakdown and sanatorium stay is vague. To Petzet he said that he had broken down at the "inquisitional hearing" in December 1945—though more probably this was in February 1946. Thereupon Kurt Beringer, the dean of the faculty of medicine, had taken him to Dr. Gebsattel. "And what did he do? He took me on a hike up through the forest in the snow. That was all. But he showed me human warmth and friendship. Three weeks later I came back a healthy man again"' (Safranski, 1998, 351–52).

2. The term *Ereignis* is one of the most famous terms to emerge from Heidegger's philosophy during the 1930s and remains crucial to Heidegger's evolving philosophical concerns for the remainder of his life. The German word is an ordinary one, which Heidegger chooses to use in an extraordinary way through his emphasis and riffing on the root *eigen* ('own'). *Ereignis* simply means 'event' in German and, while Heidegger clearly means something more than this in terms of his own usage it is worth bearing in mind that Heidegger himself didn't invent a new word but simply used an ordinary one in all sorts of innovative and experimental ways. The word 'event' doesn't really allow one to bring out some of the nuances of the way Heidegger zeros in on the root *eigen*, for example. The word *eigen* means 'own' in German, and so, Heidegger sometimes hyphenates the German word such that it would mean something like 'en-owned' (*Er-eignet*). One of the standard renderings of the term *Ereignis* has been as "the event of appropriation', and Heidegger himself would appear to have looked favourably on the French word *appropriement* as a candidate for

translating this key term of his middle and later thinking into French. The French word is related to the English word, of course; however, the French word allows one to bring out some of the connotations of 'ownness' through the root *propre* which is related to the English word 'proper', even if we tend not to think of 'proper' in quite the same way anymore. The French term can thus be used in ways that may not appear as immediately obvious in English. Notwithstanding, this key term is again an attempt to delve further into some ideas and thoughts which are already clearly in view in *Being and Time*. If one considers that Dasein is already thrown such that it has meaning, accords meanings which are given to it and finds itself such that it has already been placed in a meaningful world before and beyond its own actions or activity as an 'agent' or 'meaning-giving-subject'—then one is already on the way to what Heidegger wants to bring out with his later use of the term *Ereignis*. This is in part what lies behind some of Heidegger's discussions of the phrase *Es gibt* in *Time and Being* and the related French phrase *il y a*. The idea then would be that Dasein, for example, already finds itself as appropriated, thrown into a meaning-laden context at any given moment before it begins to reflect or abstract from its situation. This meaningfulness, then, is not the achievement of a subject or an agent any more than it was in *Being and Time*, and this is something that Heidegger is looking to reinforce and underline again and again during the course of his career. Moreover, this context within which things are revealed as meaningful, or 'are' in particular ways, is itself an epochal story. That is to say that Heidegger thinks that there is a history of these meaning-giving dispensations of being, though not to be understood as a chronological history, which culminates in the contemporary ordinance of revealing which is Enframing *(Gestell)*.

3. We know from Heinrich Petzet that Heidegger established links with Bremen as far back as 1930, shortly after he had returned to take up Husserl's chair in the University of Freiburg. According to Petzet, whose parents hosted Heidegger on that initial visit to speak at the Philosophical Society, Heidegger was surprisingly taken with the city, which was noted more for its shipping and commerce than intellectual life (see Petzet, 1993, 14–19).

4. Of course the prevailing view among certain Heideggerians is that the later work succeeds only at the expense of the deadborn and obsolete project that is *Being and Time*.

5. In *Being and Time*, Heidegger famously distinguishes between authentic death and the notions of demise and perishing. That is because Heidegger is interested in the role that our temporal limits plays in the way anything can become meaningful to or for us. Our finitude is constitutive of the manners and ways in which things can be meaningful for human beings. In order to avoid confusion, and in this he failed it seems, Heidegger looks to distinguish between this authentic notion of death, which is, ultimately a way for Dasein to be, from, for example, 'perishing'—the term which he uses again in the quoted passage to pick out the dehumanised way that the people in the death camps were put to death like so many animals on a factory farm.

6. For a more in-depth discussion of some of these issues see chapter 2 of my recently published book on the Heidegger controversy (O'Brien, 2015).

7. The term *Man* in German is used very much in the same way that we would use the term 'one' in English. 'One' might be wondering if this is a useful footnote, for example. Heidegger then uses the phrase *das Man* to pick out a public version of this impersonal pronoun which is often translated as 'the they'. A number of Heideggerians have, alas, chosen to complicate this relatively straightforward issue by insisting on using needlessly awkward renderings such as 'the anonymous anyone' when it seems pretty obvious that in the rele-

vant sections of *Being and Time* that Heidegger is thinking of *das Man* in exactly the same way that we often hear the phrase 'they' used in certain contexts in English. We regularly hear people invoke the authority of an anonymous authority in ordinary conversation and Heidegger suggests that this is very much the ordinary commonplace identity of everyday Dasein. We live our lives as part of 'the they'. 'They' say that it's not a good idea to look at a computer screen right before bedtime—and so perhaps—some of you may well be thinking of closing your tablet or laptop for the night. This is precisely the kind of use that Heidegger has in mind with the term *das Man*.

8. Heidegger quotes from Hölderlin's poem *Patmos* towards the end of his essay: 'But where danger is, grows the saving power also'.

9. The term is typically translated as 'Releasement' and is frequently associated with Heidegger's later thought; however, it is a word which is originally associated with the Medieval mystic, theologian and philosopher Meister Eckhart.

EIGHT
Heidegger 'Abroad'

FRANCE

One of the most significant developments for Heidegger, at the time of his domestic academic estrangement after the war, was the remarkable success of his efforts to ingratiate himself with French intellectuals. At the very time that the denazification committee, urged on by some Freiburg-based academics who had suffered greatly under Heidegger's rectorship, was considering stern measures against Heidegger, there were rumours of a steady stream of French intellectuals pouring into the Black Forest, looking to foster intellectual relations with Heidegger. This, in particular, outraged members of the denazification committee from the University of Freiburg and led to them insisting that the initial, rather lenient, judgement of the committee be reviewed. Heidegger was initially going to be required to take early retirement, with full Emeritus status. But, as Safranski relates

> the senate resolved to propose to the French military government that Heidegger be deprived of his teaching license and removed from his post with a reduced pension. At the end of 1946 the military government adopted this proposal and even increased its severity by ordering the discontinuation of Heidegger's pension from 1947. This decision, however, was rescinded in May 1947. (Safranski, 1998, 341)

Heidegger had already had a marked impact through the movement that came to be known as 'existentialism' in France. There is a well-known anecdote about how Raymond Aron, who was familiar with phenomenology, conveyed the rudiments of phenomenology to Sartre over cocktails at a Parisian café, explaining that phenomenology could even make the house specialty (apricot cocktails) the subject of its philosophical analysis. Sartre was so enchanted that he stopped at a Parisian bookstore on his way home and purchased a book on Husserl's phenomenology and began to devour the text in a fever of excitement. In time, Sartre became engrossed in a study of both Husserl and Heidegger. There are further reports of efforts on Heidegger's part to establish a relationship with Sartre, which the latter initially refused to reciprocate. An initial meeting was arranged but did not take place at the time[1] and, despite Heidegger's apparently sincere wish to establish a philosophical relationship with Sartre, his negative views concerning Sartre's existentialism were later famously aired in his well-known 'Letter on Humanism'.[2] The letter itself began as a response to a question from a young French philosopher, Jean Beaufret, with whom Heidegger had struck up a relationship in the postwar years. Beaufret introduced Heidegger to the poet René Char, who had been a resistance fighter during the Second World War, and the two men had an instant rapport. Char invited Heidegger to his home in Le Thor on several occasions, and during these visits, Heidegger conducted philosophical seminars attended by Beaufret and his closest students. Among these students were Francois Fédier and Francois Vezin, who were to become noted, if controversial, translators and interpreters of Heidegger's work in France.

This relationship and the tireless efforts of Beaufret to champion Heidegger's work in France were to have profound implications for French philosophy. Having already had a major impact on philosophers such as Sartre, de Beauvoir, and Levinas before and directly after the war, Heidegger became the central philosophical figure in Paris influencing a new generation of intellectuals such as Lacan, Derrida, Lyotard, Foucault, Lacoue-Labarthe, Nancy, and Irigaray to name but a few. To this day, a considerable chunk of the French philosophical scene in Paris, the beating heart of French philosophy, is indelibly marked by the influence of Heidegger, and he exercised an enormous influence on some of the great twentieth-century movements that began to dominate continental philosophy. Poststructuralism, deconstruction, hermeneutics, postmodernism, along with certain theories of art and feminism, are massively indebted to the philosophy of Heidegger, which enjoyed a period of unrivalled domination in the second half of the twentieth century in France.

This explains, in part, why the Heidegger controversy tends to generate such inflamed interest in France in particular. In Germany, for example, there is far less interest in Heidegger's philosophy than there is in France (there are some notable exceptions). For a country that is singlehandedly responsible for the philosophy of Husserl and Heidegger and the globally influential movement, phenomenology, that they helped to shape, it is remarkable that such a small proportion of the current German philosophical landscape is occupied by people working in phenomenology, never mind Heidegger. Most recently there have been attempts to diminish Heidegger's influence further, with calls to abolish chairs in Heideggerian philosophy in the few remaining outposts that still specialise in Heidegger's thought.

EASTERN THOUGHT

Heidegger engaged with a number of Eastern intellectuals who made the trip to Freiburg to meet with the famous German philosopher. Heidegger himself published a dialogue which examines some potential intersections between Japanese thought and his own evolving project.[3] Heidegger, at times, appears to be genuinely fascinated by elements of Eastern thought, and there is a significant body of secondary literature devoted to a study of the ways that some of Heidegger's core ideas intersect with Eastern thinking. Notwithstanding, Heidegger also seems wary of pursuing any such intersections in earnest, since he remains adamant that his own thought is inextricably linked to the Western tradition and that no proper philosophical conversation can take place between such different traditions. One might be forgiven for supposing that Heidegger is really only interested in exploiting certain metaphors and ideas from Eastern thought as part of an ongoing attempt to advance his own ideas concerning the history of the metaphysics of presence in Western thought. Petzet helpfully sums up some of Heidegger's views on this matter:

> Even when he knew that men like Nishitani and Tsujimura understood him, he did not let himself believe that this was generally the case in the Eastern world of thinking and teaching. In a conversation in his last years with a German religious scholar, Heidegger was sceptical about 'what his Japanese friends made out of his philosophy' and said that 'he has difficulty believing

blindly that thoughts in a language so foreign would mean the same'. (Petzet, 1993, 167)

Despite Heidegger's consistent repudiation of the prospect of any genuine and thoroughgoing cross-pollination between his thought and some of the Eastern traditions he flirted with, a vast body of secondary literature has sprung up around that precise comparative venture and it is a thriving plot within the variegated field of Heidegger interpretation today. The legitimacy or illegitimacy of such work in terms of Heidegger studies notwithstanding, it is a testament to the uniquely innovative and creative ways that Heidegger unfolded his own ideas. Heidegger proves fertile ground for readers approaching his work from a remarkable array of backgrounds.

UNITED STATES

There was little engagement with Heidegger's philosophy in North America before the end of the Second World War. Several factors contributed to Heidegger's philosophy finding yet another home away from home in the United States. One recent intellectual historian has suggested that Heidegger was initially persona non grata in the United States as a result of the foothold that analytic philosophy gained in the early 1930s with the forced emigration of some of its well-known proponents, most notably Rudolph Carnap. Carnap had already reacted strongly to Heidegger's work in a famous 1932 paper in which he tries to dismiss Heidegger's philosophical approach as bad metaphysics and as, ultimately, nonsensical. The logical positivism that Carnap brought with him was initially championed in some of the most influential philosophical centres in the United States and defended and disseminated by prominent American philosophers. At the same time, Heidegger came to be seen more and more as *the* European philosopher who had broken with the positivists and scientific philosophy more generally and was engaged instead in a shady, oracular, rhetorical posturing which could easily be put in the service of despicable political movements such as National Socialism. Of course, much of this overview is playing fast and loose with the details and intricacies of an extremely complicated and difficult story of how philosophy began to split into supposedly distinct groups, and it certainly is somewhat misleading to suggest that Heidegger was the figure who was singlehandedly responsible for the split, even if he does have a crucial role to play. One simply has to read the work of Bertrand Russell to see that figures like Nietzsche were already marked for excommunication from the 'revised' community of reputable philosophers who Russell was lobbying for. Notwithstanding, some elements of this story are useful insofar as they indicate that Heidegger was a figure who was not just obscure but was actively resisted and maligned in North American philosophical circles from the 1930s onwards.

One of the first American philosophical figures who sought to introduce Heidegger's work to the United States was John Wild:

> The Harvard and Chicago-educated Wild was not destined to be the godfather of continental philosophy in the United States, but after works such as *The Challenge of Existentialism*, that is precisely what he became. Without Wild, Heidegger's work may very well have languished in the oblivion to which Carnap's critique had supposedly sent it. It was Wild who provided some of the first academic expositions of Heidegger's thought. More importantly, however, it was Wild who orchestrated the institutional development of continental philosophy in the United States. In addition to being on the editorial board of Marvin Farber's *Philosophy and Phenomenological Research*, Wild, after leaving Harvard to take up the chairmanship of Northwestern University's philosophy department, headed up the committee that founded the Society for Phenomenology and Existential Philosophy in 1962 (a fateful year for Heidegger scholarship in the United States). SPEP, as it is commonly known, is the largest and most recognisable forum for non-analytic philosophical discussion in the United States. (Woessner, 2011, 196–97)

As Wild's interest in Heidegger deepened, he apparently even considered translating *Being and Time*:

> In a June 21, 1956, letter to Harper & Row editor Melvin Arnold, who was busy surveying the prospects for having *Sein und Zeit* translated into English, Wild explained that he and three of his students had produced a 'mimeographed translation of more than half' of *Sein und Zeit*, which he had been using in some of his Harvard courses. He gave up on translating the rest of the book, he explained, only because he had heard that the official translation rights had been granted to somebody else.
>
> The common lore has it that it was after a second visit to Europe in 1957 that Wild became convinced of Heidegger's importance. The story goes somewhat like this: Following his European excursion, he returned to Harvard and shocked his students by demanding that they drop their Aquinas and Aristotle read-

ings and immediately immerse themselves in the tasks of translating Heidegger and reading the still untranslated works of the French phenomenologist Maurice Merleau-Ponty. The 1956 letter to Harper & Row seems to prove otherwise. Ultimately, however, it matters little if Wild jumped headlong into Heidegger in 1956 or 1958. Either way, when it comes to Heidegger's American reception, Wild started the ball rolling—and thanks in large part to the efforts of those students, such as one Hubert L. Dreyfus, who helped him translate Heidegger, it has yet to come to a stop. (Woessner 2011, 197–98)

By the early 1960s, then, Heidegger's influence was beginning to be felt, despite the lack of the availability of his work in English. With the efforts of Wild and his students, and the steady trickle of discussions and publications concerning Heidegger's work alongside the eventual publication of the translation of Heidegger's most important and famous book, *Being and Time*, the trickle swelled into a torrent. And there were a few contributing factors which expedited the sudden explosion of widespread interest in Heidegger in the United States. By the time that circles interested in the work of existentialists and phenomenologists were beginning to get up and running in the early 1960s, some of Heidegger's former students were already well established in the United States. Hans Jonas, who was deeply offended by his former teacher's involvement with National Socialism, spoke at the very first meeting of what was to become the Heidegger Circle at Drew University in 1964. Some of Heidegger's most talented former students, who happened to be Jewish, were forced to emigrate to the United States to escape Nazi persecution in the 1930s and indirectly contributed to a new generation of students reading Heidegger, whose work their teachers were often responding to and, in many cases, criticising. From among these former students, it was Hannah Arendt who was again to prove one of the most significant figures for Heidegger. Arendt had emigrated to the United States in the 1930s and made a life for herself in New York, where she took up a position at the New School. Arendt, like her fellow Jewish Heidegger students, was utterly dismayed by Heidegger's actions during the 1930s; however, the former lovers began to correspond again after the war and eventually met. By this time, Arendt herself was happily married, and though there was no suggestion of any impropriety, Heidegger had since decided to confess to his wife the affair of some thirty years previous, which caused Elfride considerable distress and left her understandably suspicious of Arendt. Nevertheless, following some initial frostiness from Elfride, there appear to have been no major problems surrounding the renewed contact between Heidegger and Arendt. From this point on, Arendt visited the Heideggers frequently, and she was instrumental in arranging to have Heidegger's work translated and published in English. The relationship between Arendt and Heidegger was complicated; while she was remarkably supportive of Heidegger after the war, she was also frustrated by the fact that Heidegger clearly didn't rate her as an important philosopher in her own right. Indeed, there are suggestions that Heidegger was irritated by Arendt's philosophical success and international fame. It was characteristic of the man that he could tolerate no equals in a contemporary philosophical firmament which he wished to illuminate on his own.

Wild's student, the late Hubert Dreyfus, was to have a profound impact on the reception of Heidegger's philosophy in the United States. Dreyfus himself saw Heidegger's philosophy as opening up possibilities for philosophers working in fields typically dominated by other kinds of philosophical methodologies. As a young academic, Dreyfus subjected the work of prominent figures working in the field of artificial intelligence to robust criticisms and he further gained a reputation for making philosophers such as Heidegger intelligible to analytically oriented philosophers. Heidegger scholars are divided when it comes to their estimation of Dreyfus's interpretations of Heidegger. There is no denying his influence, however, and some of the most important and prominent scholars working on Heidegger today have been directly influenced by Dreyfus's work.

Another key figure responsible for the growing interest in Heidegger in North America was the recently deceased Father William Richardson, whose book, *Heidegger: Through Phenomenology to Thought*, came to be seen as *the* definitive study in the English-speaking world of the evolving nature of Heidegger's philosophy. Richardson met Heidegger, who was quite enthusiastic about the American doctoral candidate studying at Louvaine. Notwithstanding, Heidegger's letter to Richardson, used as a foreword to Richardson's book, clearly seeks to qualify the sense in which one may speak of a Heidegger I and a Heidegger II in ways that are in direct conflict with the central claims of some commentators (though not necessarily Richardson's). This is yet another mini-controversy within Heidegger studies that does not look likely to be resolved any time soon, and I have, I hope, said enough to indicate where my own sympathies lie on that particular issue.

The Heidegger Circle was founded in the mid- to late 1960s after a series of conferences on Heidegger's philosophy in various North American universities. The first annual meeting of the Heidegger Circle took place in 1967 at Penn State, and it has become an important intellectual association for Heidegger scholars in the United States ever since, meeting for an annual conference at a different location in early May. The Circle also now annually publishes a peer-reviewed journal (*Gatherings*) dedicated to Heidegger's philosophy. The Circle recently celebrated its fiftieth anniversary, and yet Heidegger's letters to some of the earliest gatherings stand as a stark reminder to pay due heed to the actual question that motivated Heidegger's lifelong endeavour, namely, the question concerning the *meaning* of being.

NOTES

1. Heidegger and Sartre did eventually meet briefly in Freiburg in 1952.

2. An interesting feature of volume 94 of Heidegger's *Black Notebooks* are his frequent criticisms and denunciations of existentialism. Heidegger again makes clear in these notebooks spanning much of the 1930s that *Being and Time* in no way should be conceived as an attempt to contribute to existentialism.

3. As Petzet relays in a section on Heidegger's relationship with Eastern thought, 'As early as the 1920s, Heidegger developed personal relationships with Japan. The same Count Kuki—introduced to the French language by the young tutor Jean-Paul Sartre, whom he told about Heidegger—was not the only Japanese student who then or later attended his lectures in Freiburg and contributed to his seminars. These students conveyed Heidegger's thinking back to their native country, where it was energetically taken up and sometimes understood even better than in Europe. Heidegger's writings were soon translated and read in Japanese' (Petzet, 1993, 166)

NINE
The Final Years

Ancient Greece had been something of an imaginary second home for Heidegger since the 1920s, when his engagement with Plato and Aristotle (especially Aristotle) was to have profound consequences for his thought, and continued to influence the direction of some of his most important work in the decades to come. As part of his ongoing efforts to deconstruct the history of Western ontology, Heidegger wrestled with these two towering figures from the Western tradition for extended periods before moving even further back to meditate on the fragments of the pre-Socratics. Heidegger's lectures on Plato and Aristotle from the 1920s abound with decisive philosophical insights and impulses that came to full fruition in *Being and Time*. In his later work, he struggled tirelessly with the fragments of the pre-Socratics, looking for further clues and hints as to how we might begin to understand the manner in which being can be understood as meaningful presence for human beings, and how we might have avoided being pushed onto the path of the unfolding of the metaphysics of presence. Heidegger instead wonders as to how we might have been thrown onto another path whereby being did not always have to be rendered as continuous presence. Owing to this fascination with the thinking, literature, language and culture of ancient Greece, those close to Heidegger began to hatch plans for a trip to Greece for the aging philosopher.

There were a series of aborted attempts to make the trip. Heidegger appears to have baulked at the opportunity several times before finally venturing to Greece in the early 1960s. Most likely, a combination of factors contributed to this initial reluctance. The country, which had been the idealised landscape for Heidegger's philosophical imagination for much of his adult life, was somewhere that he wanted to keep as an illusory haven for his philosophical imagination. Heidegger was clearly troubled by the possibility of disappointment at the reality of a modern-day Greece, which might pale by comparison with the glorious and quasi-mythical image of the land that dominated his imagination. Furthermore, Heidegger was unaccustomed to long journeys and, when circumstances permitted, spent most of his life as close to his beloved Black Forest as he could. There had been trips to France and Switzerland, but the borders of these countries were a stone's throw from his home and readily accessible by train. When Heidegger did finally manage to make the excursion, it appears to have been a rewarding experience. So impressed was Heidegger with his first trip to Greece that he returned in 1964, 1966 and 1967.

Heidegger's philosophical vitality was remarkable until close to the end of his life. Before he suffered a stroke, from which he made a complete recovery,[1] Heidegger was actively working on manuscripts, giving lectures, travelling to meet with other intellectuals, as well as receiving them in the hut in Todtnauberg, all the time continuing to work on new projects and ideas. The final years of Heidegger's life appear to have been peaceful and happy in the main. Heidegger and Elfride remained together throughout this time. Following his stroke, Heidegger's once frequent lecture trips and protracted periods of seclusion became a thing of the past. The Heideggers had arranged for the construction of a small apartment at the end of the garden of their home in Freiburg, which would be easier to manage in their old age. They lived in this part of the family home during the final years of Heidegger's life.

By the 1970s, Heidegger's fame extended to pretty much all parts of the globe, and he and Elfride were constantly inundated with visitors and admirers who were eager to catch a glimpse of the famous philosopher. A sign was posted outside the front door of their house in Freiburg declaring that visitors were only admitted after 5 p.m., since Heidegger still required time for his work in the mornings and early afternoons. Heidegger appears to have mellowed considerably in his old age, becoming more personable and less abrasive. He had also become something of a celebrity in his hometown of Messkirch and was frequently honoured by the local council and was made an honorary citizen.

The grace and serenity with which Heidegger faced his death is something that appears to have left a lasting impression on many people who saw him during that period. His long-time friend and admirer, Heinrich Petzet, reports that he visited Heidegger shortly before his death and found the philosopher lying in bed and talking openly about the fact that the end was near but without any fear or apprehension. The philosopher who had once devoted so much time and effort to an examination of the importance of our mortality to any sense of what it means for us to be, seems to have been calm and untroubled as the end approached.

As discussed briefly at the beginning of this book, Heidegger had famously broken all ties with the Catholic Church as a young man. Although he appeared for a time to have embraced the Protestant religion of his wife, the role that God and spirituality might have played for Heidegger is a complicated and difficult matter. Heidegger was certainly no theist in any conventional sense; nevertheless, Heidegger was also critical of atheism. Safranski relays an anecdote attributed to Max Müller which captures the ambivalence nicely:

> Max Müller reports that, on hikes, whenever they came to a church or a chapel, Heidegger always dipped his finger in the stoup and genuflected. On one occasion he had asked him if this was not inconsistent, since he had distanced himself from the dogma of the Church. Heidegger's answer had been: 'One must think historically. And where there has been so much praying, there the divine is present in a very special way'. (Safranski, 1998, 432–33)

Shortly before his death, Heidegger asked to see his one-time correspondent, the priest and theologian Bernhard Welte. Heidegger expressed a desire to have a church funeral and for Welte to speak at his graveside. Heidegger was, in the end, to have a Christian burial in the graveyard of his hometown church following his death in May 1976. In a way, Heidegger had come full circle; he returned to his hometown, the town of his birth and childhood, and was buried there. He returned to his roots in about as profound a way as is humanly possible.

NOTES

1. Apparently the only lasting effect of Heidegger's stroke was on his handwriting.

TEN
Heidegger's Legacy

Heidegger has remained as much a controversial figure in death as in life. Much of this controversy understandably stems from his association with National Socialism. The recent publication of Heidegger's *Black Notebooks* has fuelled the controversy to an even greater extent, since any and all traces of the 'official story' that Heidegger peddled after the war have now been discredited. Heidegger was a committed Nazi and an antisemite; he tried zealously to use some of the core elements of his thought to articulate a philosophy of National Socialism, for a period of time at least. Heidegger's political vision was ultimately at quite a remove from historical National Socialism, and he clearly became more and more disillusioned with the regime from the mid-1930s onwards. That is not to say, however, that his own views were unproblematic, and it is also worth bearing in mind that Heidegger was wilfully opportunistic in attempting to recklessly map the rhetoric of National Socialism onto his earlier thought in ways that simply were not legitimate. This makes the process of trying to assess the relationship between Heidegger's thinking and his commitment to National Socialism more difficult. One has to walk a tightrope between the apologists and those who dismiss Heidegger's philosophy as obscurantist Nazism.

The fact that Heidegger himself proved so mendacious and wilfully distorted and suppressed the details of his Nazi allegiances and his antisemitism exacerbates an already complicated situation. Furthermore, the drip-feeding approach, in terms of publishing some of Heidegger's more worrisome texts, only complicates matters further since it can sometimes appear as though Heidegger has a huge treasure trove of Nazi secrets stashed away when, in fact, there was a sustained period when Heidegger was actively engaged in the project of trying to articulate some kind of politically relevant philosophical position. We would have been better served by having everything revealed once and for all rather than having the controversy stoked up each time anew. Of course, in saying that Heidegger was looking to offer a sort of political philosophy, I am aware that certain Heideggerians will cite chapter and verse from some of the notebooks where Heidegger is clearly critical of any attempt to produce a philosophy of National Socialism. However one wants to split hairs, the fact remains that Heidegger genuinely believed he could be the spiritual and philosophical Führer of an awakening in Germany[1] that would change the course of history in Europe and the Western world in general, and perhaps across the planet, given the colonial reach of the West. He believed that National Socialism represented a genuine political platform from which his ideas might come into effect.

Despite the problems facing anyone interested in the continuing relevance of Heidegger's thought, it is a mistake to dismiss his work as just so much Nazi ideology, as Faye and his supporters do. But we must also avoid the temptation to diminish the relationship between Heidegger's philosophy and his politics out of existence, since that serves to sanitise some of the more problematic elements of his thought. We should remain wary of the implications of his attempts to resist modernity in radical ways. Heidegger remained a staunch enemy of democracy and liberalism in any and all of its forms. Despite the disastrous consequences of his attempts to articulate a political philosophy and to enter the political fray, Heidegger never, in fact, fully relinquished his views. Some might see this as bloody-minded stubbornness, further proof of his vainglory or hubris; others might want to credit Heidegger with a kind of consistency on this issue. Whatever way one looks at this question, it should surely give us pause. We find Heidegger again making overtly political statements in his later philosophy in ways that are deeply problematic in the context of postwar Germany:

> Then we notice that a work of art has flowered in the ground of our homeland. As we hold this simple fact in mind, we cannot help remembering at once that during the last two centuries great poets and thinkers have been brought forth from the Swabian

land. Thinking about it further makes clear at once that Central Germany is likewise such a land, and so are East Prussia, Silesia, and Bohemia.

We grow thoughtful and ask: does not the flourishing of any genuine work depend upon its roots in a native soil? (DT, 47)

Heidegger goes on to lament the plight of his fellow Germans in the aftermath of the Second World War.

Many Germans have lost their homeland, have had to leave their villages and towns, have been driven from their native soil. (DT, 48)

Owing to Heidegger's belief in the unique destiny of the German people in terms of their capacity to save the West from a technological apocalypse, he insists that what is needed is 'a life-giving homeland in whose ground man may stand rooted, that is, be autochthonic' (DT, 48). In his recently published notebooks from the 1930s and 1940s, we find Heidegger stressing again and again the salvific vocation of the German people in the face of what he perceives to be a planetary crisis of technology. This vision dovetails with his commitment to a rather bizarre cocktail of his own unique history of Western metaphysics and a rampant Nationalism which is often not much more than a rather crude provincialism. If we then consider the seemingly innocuous finale to his interview with *Der Spiegel* in 1966, we can see just how entrenched Heidegger's commitment to his own contentious views of the 1930s was:

S: You assign in particular a special task to the Germans?

H: Yes, in the sense of a dialogue with Hölderlin.

S: Do you believe the Germans have a special qualification for this reversal?

H: I have in mind the inner relationship of the German language with the language of the Greeks and with their thought. This has been confirmed for me today again by the French. When they begin to think, they speak German, being sure that they could not make it with their own language.

('Only a God Can Save Us', 113)

Other aspects of the controversy surrounding Heidegger's thought owe more to an unfortunate development in twentieth-century philosophy, which has led to something of a phony war between so-called analytic and Continental philosophy. Without getting too bogged down in the history of this particular divide, Heidegger is often portrayed as the arch-villain for having led philosophy astray through his promotion of ambiguity, imprecision, a lack of rigour and the proliferation of jargon, mysticism and bad poetry masquerading as philosophical profundity. Admittedly, Heidegger, and some other prominent philosophers in the Continental tradition, have inspired some rather unfortunate disciples who don't seem to understand that their 'heroes' did not write obscure prose or 'bad poetry' for the sake of it, nor did they lack rigour or training. Rather, some of the subjects they tackled demanded particular styles or approaches.

In terms of identifying the most important philosopher of the twentieth century, any attempt to single out one figure is always going to be controversial. In the end, such evaluations are pointless. It makes about as much sense as trying to argue that Messi is a better footballer than Ronaldo, or that Joyce is the greatest novelist of the twentieth century. For some people, Wittgenstein is by far and away the most important philosopher of the twentieth century, others insist that the laurels should go to Husserl. Others might make a plausible case for some other philosophers. However, if one simply wanted to identify the philosopher who has had the widest possible *influence* in the last one hundred years, it seems obvious that Heidegger is considerably further ahead of anyone else. That is not a value judgement concerning the superiority of Heidegger's philosophy over any other thinker. It is simply a fact that Heidegger's philosophy has had a profound and lasting influence, and not just on subsequent generations of philosophers; his influence has seeped into all kinds of fields and disciplines in a way that just does not seem to be true of any other twentieth-century thinker.

It is hard to tell what kind of future lies in store for Heidegger studies. When the *Black Notebooks* were originally published, many philosophers, some of them Heideggerians, were confidently predicting the death of Heideggerian philosophy. The revelations to be found in the notebooks, they insisted, signalled the death knell for a philosophy that could ill afford to be blighted any further by controversy or scandal. Reports and prognoses concerning the imminent demise of Heidegger studies have turned out to be greatly exaggerated, alarmist and unfounded. As things stand, the notebooks have not shown Heidegger's philosophy to be corrupt beyond redemption, and while the controversy rages on, few respectable philosophers or scholars still maintain that the end of Heidegger's reign as one of the most important thinkers of the twentieth century is at an end. That is not to say that the Heidegger controversy will fizzle out over time. In many ways, it is only truly beginning, as scholars face squarely the question of how to read the texts of a thinker whose work, while not reducible to National Socialism, was nevertheless twisted and manipulated in various ways owing to his own belief that a happy union could be forged between his own thought and the new awakening in Germany which he initially saw as an underlying possibility of National Socialism.

Whatever one's personal feelings might be about this terribly complicated and controversial philosopher, and regardless of how dangerous some of his philosophical, cultural and political leanings might be, one simple and incontrovertible fact remains: Martin Heidegger is one of the most original and creative philosophers to have lived and worked in the twentieth century. Any curriculum or philosophical education which does not include some kind of engagement with his work is all the more impoverished as a consequence. Heidegger was a philosopher and scholar of the first rank, the breadth of his work is staggering, and such was his level of erudition and industry that he managed to make decisive contributions to the study of numerous philosophers in the Western tradition, including but not limited to, the pre-Socratics, Plato, Aristotle, Augustine, Leibniz, Kant, Hegel, Schelling and Nietzsche. In many cases, such is the originality and profundity of Heidegger's engagement with these thinkers that even specialists, poorly disposed towards Heidegger's own philosophy, find themselves unwittingly indebted to the influence he had on the way interpretations and understandings of these thinkers developed and evolved.[2] This is not to suggest that Heidegger was a mere historian of philosophy; rather, his influence in this regard is the result of his lifelong attempt to work through and wrestle with the tradition he himself belonged to. He wanted to trace the history of Western metaphysics back to its origin before then embarking on the project of finding a new beginning which might be free from the stifling and stultifying constraints of the metaphysics of presence.

Reading Heidegger is challenging for even the most accomplished philosopher. He pushes the boundaries of language further than anyone before or since in his attempt to get beyond the metaphysical constraints he believes traditional language is tethered by, and the result is often the most impenetrable and tortuous philosophical prose imaginable. At a time when much of what we see and read is constantly modified and simplified for quick and easy consumption, Heidegger's writings might seem like an outrage against the artificial simplicity which has become *de rigeur*, even in the academy. One has to imagine that Heidegger himself might not be displeased at just how alien his work must seem within such a culture; after all, he was already bemoaning the influence of a certain 'journalistic' packaging of anything that required time and patience for careful reflection and analysis. To read Heidegger is a daunting undertaking. There are no easy or cheap thrills. His work does not repay quick reading or skimming. He makes extreme demands of his readers. However, for those of you willing to undertake these philosophical voyages with him, those of you willing to stay the course, often going for long stretches with little hope of illumination or respite, simply page after page of sometimes turgid, gnarled philosophical terrain, with no shortcuts or easy passages around mountains or marshes, for those determined few, the rewards are extraordinary. Such readers will soon begin to see why so many intellectuals have found their thinking and their lives changed irrevocably after voyaging through one text or another with Martin Heidegger.

NOTES

1. As Ott recounts, 'In the weeks preceding the rectorship address rector Heidegger was already establishing a new set of ground rules. He had no intention, for example, of convening the Senate to discuss the major problems associated with *Gleichschaltung*. As far as he was concerned, the University had already been "co-ordinated" and "brought into line" (*gleichgeschaltet*). It had, in other words, been made subservient to the "leadership principle" (*Fuehrerprinzip*), to which the only appropriate response was obedience, not corporate democracy—an outdated and crumbling edifice, no longer capable of supporting the weight of the new. For this reason he was quite indifferent to the extreme degree of ill-feeling he provoked. . . . Eucken made his feelings known to the pro-rector Sauer, who noted the incident in his diary: "He said that Heidegger was acting as though he wanted to run the whole show himself, on the principle of the *Fuehrer* system. He obviously saw himself as the natural philosopher and intellectual leader of the movement—and as the only great thinker since Heraclitus." Eucken had certainly put his finger on it, characterising Heidegger's view of himself with remarkable accuracy and defining the extent of his intellectual-political ambitions' (Ott, 1993, 169).

2. As Arendt recalls, 'Plato was not talked *about* and his theory of Ideas expounded; rather for an entire semester a single dialogue was pursued and subjected to question step by step, until the time-honored doctrine had disap-

peared to make room for a set of problems of immediate and urgent relevance. Today this sounds quite familiar, because nowadays so many proceed this way; but no one did so before Heidegger' (Arendt, 1971, 3).

Sources

Arendt, Hannah. 'Martin Heidegger at Eighty'. Translated by Albert Hofstadter. *The New York Review of Books*. 21 October 1971.
Bernasconi, Robert. 'Another Eisenmenger'. In *Heidegger's Black Notebooks: Responses to Antisemitism*. Edited by Andrew J. Mitchell and Peter Trawny. New York: Columbia University Press, 2017.
Carnap, Rudolf. 'The Elimination of Metaphysics through Logical Analysis of Language'. Translated by Arthur Pap. *Erkenntnis*, vol. 2 (1932).
Dahlstrom, Daniel O. *The Heidegger Dictionary*. London: Bloomsbury, 2013.
Derrida, Jacques. 'Philosopher's Hell: An Interview'. In *The Heidegger Controversy: A Critical Reader*. Edited by Richard Wolin. New York: Columbia University Press, 1991.
Ettinger, Elzbieta. *Hannah Arendt/Martin Heidegger*. New Haven, CT: Yale University Press, 1995.
Farias, Victor. *Heidegger and Nazism*. French materials translated by Paul Burrell, with the advice of Dominic Di Bernardi. German materials translated by Gabriel R. Ricci. Philadelphia, PA: Temple University Press, 1989.
Faye, Emmanuel. *Heidegger: The Introduction of Nazism into Philosophy*. Translated by Michael B. Smith. New Haven, CT: Yale University Press, 2009.
Fichte, Johann Gottlieb. *Beiträge zur Berichtigung der Urteile des Publicums über die franzoeische Revolution*. (Ed. R. Schottke. Hamburg, 1973. 114ff.) Passages taken from Paul Lawrence Rose. *German Question/Jewish Question: Revolutionary Antisemitism from Kant to Wagner*. Princeton, NJ: Princeton University Press, 1992.
Gadamer, Hans-Georg. *Heidegger's Ways*. Translated by John W. Stanley. Albany: State University of New York Press, 1994.
———. *Hermeneutics between History and Philosophy*, vol. 1. Edited and Translated by Pol Vandevelde and Arun Iyer. London: Bloomsbury, 2016.
Hawking, Stephen, and Leonard Mlodinow. *The Grand Design*. New York: Bantam Books, 2010.
Käufer, Stephan. 'On Heidegger on Logic'. *Continental Philosophy Review* 34 (2001): 455–76.
Marcuse, Herbert. 'An Exchange of Letters'. In *The Heidegger Controversy: A Critical Reader*. Cambridge, MA: MIT Press, 1993.
Merleau-Ponty, Maurice. 'Eye and Mind'. In *The Merleau-Ponty Aesthetics Reader: Philosophy and Painting*. Edited by Galen A. Johnson. Evanston, IL: Northwestern University Press, 1993.
O'Brien, Mahon. *Heidegger, History and the Holocaust*. London: Bloomsbury, 2015.
Ott, Hugo. *Martin Heidegger: A Political Life*. Translated by Allan Blunden. London: HarperCollins, 1993.
Petzet, Heinrich. *Encounters and Dialogues with Martin Heidegger 1929–1976*. Translated by Parvis Emad and Kenneth Maly. Chicago: University of Chicago Press, 1993.

Redner, Harry. 'Philosophy and Antisemitism'. *Modern Judaism* 22, no. 2 (May 2002). 115–41.
Richardson, William J. *Heidegger: Through Phenomenology to Thought*. New York: Fordham University Press, 1993.
Rockmore, Tom. 'Heidegger after Trawny'. In *Heidegger's Black Notebooks: Responses to Antisemitism*. Edited by Andrew J. Mitchell and Peter Trawny. New York: Columbia University Press, 2017.
Rose, Paul Lawrence. *German Question/Jewish Question: Revolutionary Antisemitism from Kant to Wagner*. Princeton, NJ: Princeton University Press, 1992.
Safranski, Rüdiger. *Martin Heidegger: Between Good and Evil*. Translated by Ewald Osers. Cambridge, MA: Harvard University Press, 1998.
Sheehan, Thomas. 'Emmanuel Faye: The Introduction of Fraud into Philosophy?' *Philosophy Today* 59, no. 3 (Summer 2015): 367–400.
———. *Making Sense of Heidegger*. London: Rowman & Littlefield International, 2014.
Sluga, Hans. *Heidegger's Crisis: Philosophy and Politics in Nazi Germany*. Cambridge, MA: Harvard University Press, 1993.
Trawny, Peter. *Heidegger and the Myth of a Jewish World Conspiracy*. Translated by Andrew J. Mitchell. Chicago: University of Chicago Press, 2015.
van Buren, John. *The Young Heidegger: Rumor of the Hidden King*. Bloomington: Indiana University Press, 1994.
Woessner, Martin. *Heidegger in America*. Cambridge: Cambridge University Press, 2011.

WORKS BY HEIDEGGER

'A Letter from Heidegger'. Translated by W. J. Richardson, S. J. In *Heidegger and the Quest for Truth*. Edited by Manfred S. Frings. Chicago: Quadrangle Books, 1968.
Basic Concepts of Aristotelian Philosophy. Translated by Robert D. Metcalf and Mark B. Tanzer. Bloomington: Indiana University Press, 2009.
BFL—Martin Heidegger. *Bremen and Freiburg Lectures: Insight into That Which Is and Basic Principles of Thinking*. Translated by Andrew J. Mitchell. Bloomington: Indiana University Press, 2012.
BT—Martin Heidegger. *Being and Time*. Translated by John Macquarrie and Edward Robinson. Oxford: Blackwell Publishing, 1962.
BW—*Basic Writings*. Edited by David Farrell Krell. London, Routledge, 1993.
CP—*Contributions to Philosophy (From Enowning)*. Translated by Parvis Emad and Kenneth Maly. Bloomington: Indiana University Press, 1999.
DT—*Discourse on Thinking*. Translated by John M. Anderson and E. Hans Freund. New York: Harper & Row, 1966.
IM—*Introduction to Metaphysics*. Translated by Gregory Fried and Richard Polt. New Haven, CT: Yale University Press, 2000.
LW—Martin Heidegger. *Martin Heidegger: Letters to His Wife 1915–1970*. Selected, edited and annotated by Gertrud Heidegger. Translated by R. D. V. Glasgow. Cambridge, MA: Polity Press, 2008.
NHS—*Nature, History, State*. Translated and edited by Gregory Fried and Richard Polt. New York: Bloomsbury, 2015.
'Only a God Can Save Us'. In *The Heidegger Controversy: A Critical Reader*. Edited by Richard Wolin. Cambridge, MA: MIT Press, 1993.

PM— *Pathmarks*. Edited by William McNeill. Cambridge: Cambridge University Press, 1998.
OTB—*On Time and Being*. Translated by Joan Stanbaugh. New York: Harper & Row, 1972.
OWA—'Origin of the Work of Art'. In *The Heidegger Reader*. Edited by Günter Figal. Bloomington: Indiana University Press, 2009.
Ponderings II–VI: Black Notebooks 1931–38. Translated by Richard Rojcewicz. Bloomington: Indiana University Press, 2016.
Ponderings VII–XI: Black Notebooks 1938–1939. Translated by Richard Rojcewicz. Bloomington: Indiana University Press, 2017.
Ponderings XII–XV: Black Notebooks 1939–1941. Translated by Richard Rojcewicz. Bloomington: Indiana University Press, 2017.
QCT—*The Question Concerning Technology and Other Essays*. Translated by William Lovitt. New York: Harper & Row, 1977.
'The Rectorate 1933/34: Facts and Thoughts'. Translated by Karsten Harries. *Review of Metaphysics* 38, no. 3 (March 1985).
WP—'Why Do I Stay in the Provinces'. In *Heidegger: The Man and the Thinker*. Edited by Thomas Sheehan. Chicago: Precedent Publishing, 1981.

Index

absence, 30–34, 40–41, 46–49, 94
Adorno, Theodor, 7, 16n1
alêtheia , 57
angst, 46
antisemitism, 14, 16n4, 17n12, 58, 61, 62–63, 68n4, 71–72, 74, 75–76, 78n9, 111
anxiety, 46, 52n10
Arendt, Hannah, 22–23, 71–72, 105, 116n2
Aristotle, 1, 7, 13, 16n7, 21, 29–30, 42, 103, 107, 115
art, 40, 50, 64–67, 77n7, 79, 100, 112
authentic, 36, 46, 65, 68n4, 83, 96n5; authenticity, 16n1

being-in-the-world, 44, 45, 49
Beaufret, Jean, 56, 57, 100
Beauvoir, Simone de, 100
Bernasconi, Robert, 69n6, 69n7
Black Notebooks, xin1, xiin4, 58, 59, 63, 73, 76, 77n5, 106n2, 111, 114
Bremen, 80, 81, 96n3
Brentano, Franz, 5n1, 16n7, 19

Cassirer, Ernst, 24n2
care, 46, 63
Carnap, Rudolf, 33, 35, 51n3, 51n5, 103
Char, Rene, 92, 100
clearing, 4, 32–33
concern, 44–46, 52n10
conservative, 71

das Man (the they), 83, 96n7
Dasein, 3, 5n3, 31, 39, 42–43, 46–50, 52n6–52n7, 52n9–53n11, 94, 95n1–95n2, 96n5, 96n7
death, 11, 46, 82, 83, 96n5
democracy, 14–15, 74, 112, 116n1
Derrida, Jacques, 100
Dreyfus, Hubert, 103–105

Enframing (*Gestell*), 80–83, 87–89, 92–95, 95n2
ethnic chauvinism, 56, 74, 78n9
everyday (everydayness), 3, 24n1, 24n4, 40–48, 52n7, 52n10, 83–85, 96n7
existentialism, ix, 43–50, 99, 103, 106n2

Farias, Victor, 72–73
Faye, Emmanuel, xin2, xin3, 68n4, 73, 112
Fichte, Johann Gottlieb, 60–62, 67n2, 68n4, 68n5, 69n6
Freiburg, ix, 9, 12–15, 16n3, 16n6, 20, 27, 30, 50, 56, 71, 76, 96n3, 99, 101, 106n1, 106n3, 108

Gadamer, Hans Georg, 22, 67
Gelassenheit (Releasement), 74, 77n7, 79, 93–95
Gröber, Conrad, 13, 16n6

Hawking, Stephen, 88–89
Heidegger, Elfride, 8–9, 14–15, 16n3, 105, 108
Heidegger, Fritz, 14, 17n9, 77n1
Heraclitus, 63, 116n1
hermeneutics, ix, 20–21, 24n4, 42, 100
hermeneutic circle, 42, 51n4

history, 20, 21, 64–66, 91, 94, 95n2
historicity, 91, 94
historical, 3, 8, 9, 20–21, 31, 34, 41, 48, 58, 64, 66, 75, 78n9, 109
Hitler, Adolf, 77n1
Hölderlin, Friedrich, 15, 55, 64–67, 113
Holocaust, 81, 82
humanism, 63
Husserl, Edmund, ix, 1, 5n1, 8, 16n7, 19, 21–22, 24n1–24n2, 27, 42, 50, 71–72, 100, 114

idealism, 68n5
intentionality, 24n1, 40, 43
Irigaray, Luce, 100

Jaspers, Karl, 21–22
Jonas, Hans, 72, 77n3, 104
Jünger, Ernst, 80

Kant, Immanuel, 1, 5n1, 8, 24n2, 68n4, 68n5, 115

Lacoue-Labarthe, Phillipe, 100
Leibniz, G. W., 32, 115
liberalism, 15, 112
logic, 21, 32, 34–37, 51n5
Löwith, Karl, 22, 72, 77n3, 77n5

Marburg, 19–23, 24n3, 27, 42
Marcuse, Herbert, 72, 77n3
Merleau-Ponty, Maurice, 91, 103
Messkirch, 7, 9, 17n9, 79, 108
metaphysics, 20, 30–34, 40–41, 46–50, 52n9, 58, 61, 63–67, 68n4, 80, 87, 92–94, 101–103, 107, 113, 115
modernity, 7, 58–60, 64, 77n7, 112
mood, 34, 46, 52n10, 53n11

National Socialism, ix, 62–63, 71–72, 75–76, 77n7, 102, 104, 111–112, 114

Nazi, ix–xi, 16n1, 17n12, 61, 71–72, 75–76, 77n2, 77n7–78n8, 79, 83, 99, 104, 111–112
neo-Kantian, 20–21, 24n2, 51n5
negation, 35
Nietzsche, Friedrich, 20, 67, 102, 115
nothing, 30–40, 46–48, 51n5, 52n10
nullity, 35

ontology (ontological), 3, 45, 48–50, 94, 107
Ott, Hugo, 63, 72, 77n4, 116n1

Petzet, Heinrich, 11–12, 16n4, 16n5, 17n9, 55–57, 95n1, 96n3, 101, 106n3, 109
phenomenology, ix, 1–2, 5n1, 16n7, 19–22, 24n2, 42–50, 52n10, 65, 71, 91, 99–100, 103–104
Plato, 29–30, 48, 87, 107, 115, 116n2
poetry, 20–21, 55, 57, 64, 66–67, 79, 92–95
Polt, Richard, 76
possibility, 35, 37–40, 46–50
presence, 30–33, 34, 37, 40–45, 48–50, 87–88, 92–94, 107;
  metaphysics of, 33–34, 40, 46–48, 58–61, 63, 65, 67, 87, 92, 101, 107, 115
pre-Socratics, 29, 107, 115

Releasement (*Gelassenheit*), 77n7, 79, 93, 97n9
Resoluteness (*Entschlossenheit*), 93
Richardson, William, 4–5, 5n2, 49, 105–106
Rockmore, Tom, 68n4
roots, 10, 63, 68n4, 77n7, 92, 109, 112–113; rootedness, 10, 77n7

Safranski, Rudiger, 9, 22, 95n1, 99, 109
Sartre, Jean-Paul, 99–100, 106n1, 106n3
Spengler, Oswald, 80

standing reserve, 82, 89
Strauss, Leo, 22, 72
Streicher, Julius, 71, 77n2
subjectivity, 3, 29, 48

technology, x, 29, 61, 74, 79–85, 87–89, 92–93, 113
temporality, 4, 21, 42
thrownness (*Geworfenheit*), 5n3, 34, 43, 48–50, 53n11, 95n2, 107
time, 4, 20–21, 24n1, 29, 42–50, 66, 86, 94
Todtnauberg, 11, 16n3, 17n9, 67, 108
tradition, ix, 27, 30–32, 34, 35–36, 37, 40, 55, 59–62, 67, 101–102, 107, 115
transcendence, 52n10
transcendental, 19–21, 24n1, 42, 50
Trawny, Peter, xiin4, 16n2, 68n3, 68n4, 73, 78n9
truth (See also *Aletheia*), 2–4, 21, 33, 50, 57–58, 63, 66; correspondence theory of, 58
turn (*Kehre*), 28, 80–81

Wild, John, 103–104
Wolin, Richard, 57, 72–74
world, 21, 24n1, 40, 42–50, 52n10, 57–59, 62, 64–67, 74, 85–86, 88–91, 95n2

www.ingramcontent.com/pod-product-compliance
Lightning Source LLC
Chambersburg PA
CBHW021859230426
43671CB00006B/451